CW01395022

TAKING THE TRAIN

Two Centuries of Railway Travel

TAKING THE TRAIN

Two Centuries of Railway Travel

Anthony Burton

First published in Great Britain in 2024 by
Pen and Sword Transport
An imprint of
Pen & Sword Books Ltd.
Yorkshire - Philadelphia

ISBN 978 1 39903 670 2

A CIP catalogue record for this book is available from the British Library.

Typeset in 11.5/14 pt Palatino by SJmagic DESIGN SERVICES, India.

Printed and bound in the UK on paper from a sustainable source by CPI Group (UK) Ltd., Croydon. CR0 4YY.

Pen & Sword Books Ltd. incorporates the imprints of Pen & Sword Books: After the Battle, Archaeology, Atlas, Aviation, Battleground, Discovery, Family History, History, Maritime, Military, Naval, Politics, Railways, Select, Transport, True Crime, Fiction, Frontline Books, Leo Cooper, Praetorian Press, Seaforth Publishing, Wharncliffe and White Owl.

For a complete list of Pen & Sword titles please contact

PEN & SWORD BOOKS LIMITED
George House, Units 12 & 13, Beevor Street, Off Pontefract Road,
Barnsley, South Yorkshire, S71 1HN, England
E-mail: enquiries@pen-and-sword.co.uk
Website: www.pen-and-sword.co.uk

or

PEN AND SWORD BOOKS
1950 Lawrence Rd, Havertown, PA 19083, USA
E-mail: uspen-and-sword@casematepublishers.com
Website: www.penandswordbooks.com

CONTENTS

Chapter 1

BEGINNINGS

When did passengers first start travelling by train? That is not quite such a simple question to answer as one might think. 'Taking the train' implies passengers are heading for a destination and trains, by definition, cannot consist of just a single carriage. That means we can rule out Trevithick's pioneering attempt to secure funding for railway locomotives, when he invited people to ride round a circular track in London in a carriage hauled by his locomotive *Catch-me-who-can*. Earlier in 1804 he had built an engine that was intended to carry goods between the Penydarren iron works at Merthyr Tydfil and the Glamorganshire Canal at Abercynon. The line on which it ran was just one of many such lines that had been built in Britain, mainly in the eighteenth and early nineteenth centuries, usually known as tramways or plateways. They all served the same general purpose, joining an industrial concern, often a colliery, to a navigable river or canal. Why were they built? The answer to that can be found in a set of eighteenth-century experiments, designed to find how much load a horse could pull in different circumstances. The least efficient way was to put a load on the horse's back and that could be improved by having the horse pull a cart, but given the dreadful state of many of the roads of the time it was not a great improvement. A railed track made a big difference – but that was still not as effective as having the horse pull a boat on a river or canal. The tramways were effective links and were privately owned and financed – there was no thought of using them for passenger travel at first.

The situation changed in 1804 when parliament passed an Act for a line from the Swansea Canal to stone quarries at Oystermouth. It was to go through a few name changes, but the one generally agreed is the Swansea and Mumbles Railway. The Act specified that it could be used for wagons and carriages, pulled by men, horses or 'otherwise' – with no

indication of what the 'otherwise' might entail. And although Trevithick had already demonstrated his steam locomotive, the line opened as just another tramway, hauling goods in horse-drawn wagons. Then in 1807, a local man offered to pay the company £20 per annum for the right to run a passenger coach on the line. It was a single coach, not a train of coaches, but it was the first regular passenger service to be run on a railway, having two return trips a day, with a single ticket costing one shilling. The carriage itself carried sixteen passengers altogether, and had a wooden body on an iron frame, carried on iron wheels.

This is a very poor quality photograph, but it is included because of its historic significance. It shows the Swansea and Oystermouth Railway, the world's first to operate a regular passenger service, in the days when everything was horse drawn. Steam locomotives would be added later.

A few accounts have survived of travelling in this vehicle. In 1808, a Miss Spence took a ride to Oystermouth and declared she had 'never spent an afternoon with more delight'. She was clearly made of sterner stuff than Richard Ayton, who described his experiences in his book *A Voyage round Great Britain in the year 1815.* He noted that the carriage trundled along at little more than a walking pace to the accompaniment of the noise of 'twenty sledge hammers at full play'. The passengers were bounced around inside the carriage 'in a state of dizziness and confusion of the sense that it is well if he recovers from in a week'. Eventually, the line would be worked by steam locomotives, and the holiday trade taking the citizens of Swansea out to the seaside and the beautiful Gower peninsula became far more important than the trade in lugging blocks of stone. However, in its early manifestation, it can hardly be said to carry passenger trains, so we have to move forward again in time.

The early years of the nineteenth century saw the gradual introduction of basic steam locomotives on colliery lines in North East England. The lines themselves were still privately owned and there was no question of them being used for anything other than shifting coal. In 1821, however, a new line was proposed that would link collieries to the River Tees at Stockton, which would be a public railway. It was called the Stockton & Darlington, which was a little misleading, as Darlington is only half way down the line that actually extended to a colliery at Witton. So, although the name might have suggested a route designed to join two towns, it was actually just another colliery line writ large. Two years later, however, the company applied for a second Act of Parliament. The Stockton & Darlington Railway Act of 1823 contained two very important phrases. Firstly, that the company were allowed to 'make and use locomotives thereon' and secondly that they could charge 6d per mile for 'every description of carriage, waggon, or cart, which shall be used for the conveyance of passengers or parcels'. It was the first public railway authorised in this way. Was this a real starting point? It could be argued that it was, but again we have to apply a caveat – how was the line actually run, when it opened for business?

The opening ceremony took place on 27 September 1825. A special train was to be run, starting near the western

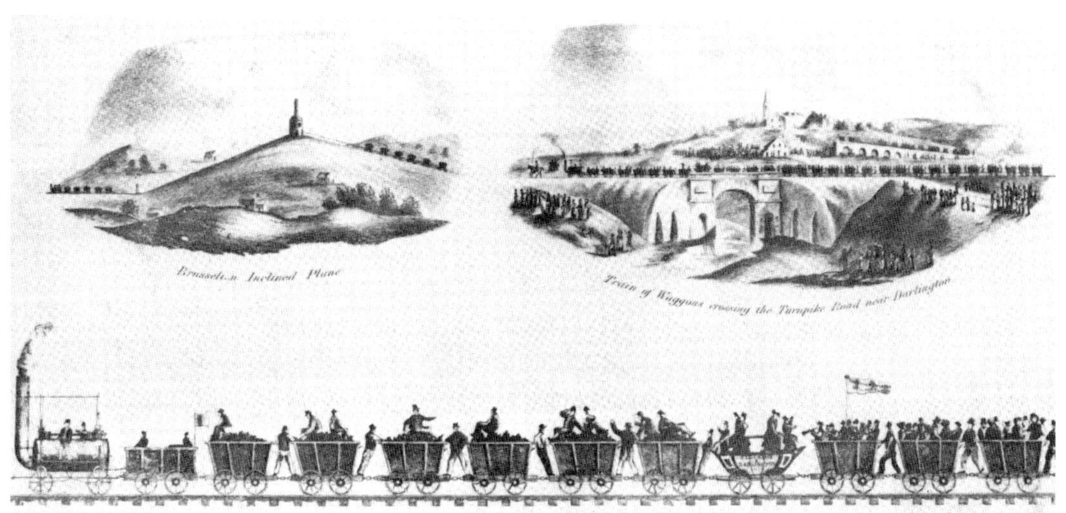

Three views of the opening of the Stockton & Darlington in a lithograph by J. Bousefield. The picture top left shows the Brusselton incline where the procession started. Trucks are being moved up and down the incline, hauled by a stationary steam engine at the top of the hill. The procession can be seen setting off at the left of the picture.

end of the line, hauled by the new locomotive, *Locomotion*. Behind it were six wagons of coal, then the company's coach, *Experiment*, which was an ordinary stage coach, but fitted with iron, flanged wheels. This was occupied by the proprietors. Then came six more wagons, fitted with seats for the gentry and finally another fourteen wagons with standing room only for everyone else. The procession was led by a man on a horse carrying a pennant. Curiously, the illustration above, although made at the time, does not show the coach. The event drew huge enthusiastic crowds as described in the newspaper, the *Courant*.

> The signal being given, the engine started off with this immense train of carriages, and here the scene became most interesting, the horsemen galloping across the fields to accompany the engine and the people on foot running on each side of the road, endeavouring to keep up with the cavalcade. The railway descending with a gentle inclination towards Darlington, though not uniform, the rate of speed was consequently variable. On the part of the railway it was intended to ascertain at what rate of speed the engine could travel with safety. In some parts the speed was frequently 12 miles per hour, and in one place, for short distance, near Darlington, 15 miles per hour, and at that time the number of passengers was counted to 450,

> which, together, with the coals, merchandise, and carriages could amount to nearly 90 tons.

The Scotsman also described the event: 'Nothing could exceed the beauty and grandeur of the scene. Throughout the whole distance the fields and lanes were covered with elegantly dressed females and all descriptions of spectators.' The most striking event came, however, when the train ran alongside a road and a stage coach, when the passengers could see 'the striking contrast exhibited by the power of the engine and the horse – the engine with her 600 passengers and the load and the coach with four horses and only 16 passengers'. There was no doubt that the sight of this train full of passengers – whether 600 or the more modest 450 – was greeted with huge enthusiasm. But once the excitement of the opening day had died down, the celebratory feast had been eaten and the toasts drunk, the railway began its actual working life. It was to be very different.

The main business of the line had always been to carry coal, but a passenger service was also begun in October 1825 between Stockton and Darlington, using the company coach that had featured in the opening cavalcade. It ran six days a week, sometime twice a day, sometimes just the one return journey – and never on Sundays. The fare was one shilling and the journey took 2½ hours on the uphill route from Stockton and 2 hours on the return. As the distance between the two is only about 13 miles, this is not the dashing 12 miles an hour of the first train. But the coach was not attached to a steam locomotive – it was pulled by horses. The only advantage it had over other coaches was that it enjoyed a smoother ride than one on the road and required less effort from the horses. The passenger train as we know it today had not arrived yet after all.

The Stockton & Darlington did, however, offer a real starting point. It had shown that there was a huge public interest in the novelty of travelling on a steam railway and entrepreneurs began to see the financial implications of developing the whole idea. One enthusiast for railway construction was William James, a land agent from Henley-in-Arden. He attempted to interest investors in a line to link Stratford-on-Avon to London, but only succeeded in promoting a tramway from Stratford to Moreton-in-Marsh. Undeterred, he came up with a new idea – a line to link Liverpool to Manchester. This made far more sense. Liverpool had become the major port for the import of cotton from America and Manchester was the heart of the cotton industry. Goods between the two centres had previously been mainly moved by water via the Bridgewater Canal, the proprietors of which were keen to stop the competition for their trade. James and his supporters argued that the canal was serving them badly: 'It will be shown that … goods have taken twenty-one days in coming from America to Liverpool, and that they have staid upon the wharfs before they could get conveyance to Manchester for more than six weeks.' The promoters of the railway were equally aware that there was a steady flow of business men also travelling the same route The arguments between the two sides were battled out in the courts. But there was another argument going on at the same time between the railway supporters. All agreed a railed track was needed, but how was it to be worked?

The obvious answer might seem to be – with steam locomotives. But the experiences of traffic on the Stockton & Darlington was only with slow moving coal trains – and though the engine might have made a sprightly 12 miles an hour going downhill, it had puffed and wheezed to a much slower pace going uphill and had sometimes stopped altogether. Would a similar service lure customers away from the familiar stagecoach? So, while one faction did favour locomotives, another preferred having a set of stationary steam engines set up along the route, hauling trains from one to the other by cables. Eminent engineers were sent to look at the existing services and came back not very impressed by what they saw of locomotive performance. The engineer George Stephenson, however, put up a compelling case for the locomotive. Eventually it was decided to hold a trial to see if a locomotive could be designed that would have the sort of performance that would make a passenger railway successful. The requirement was that a 6-ton engine had to cover the equivalent of whole distance between Manchester and Liverpool on a level track with a 20-ton train at an average

The opening of the Canterbury and Whitstable railway seen from the tunnel. On this section of the approach to Canterbury, the train is being hauled uphill by a stationary engine.

speed of 10mph, using steam pressure that was not to exceed 50 pounds per square inch (psi). Entrants could also present a 4½ ton engine, with slightly less stringent requirements. This is not the place to go into the details of how the trial that was held on a length of track at Rainhill went, but sufficient to say that the winning entry was the *Rocket,* designed by Robert Stephenson that more than met the standards required – and was the only competitor to do so. The result was the decision was taken that the line would be run by locomotives.

The story of the years leading up to the opening of the Liverpool & Manchester is a complex one of failures and successes, arguments and quarrels and one of the victims was the man who had started it all, William James. His enthusiasm had overtaken his financial common sense, and as a result his business had suffered from neglect. He was made bankrupt and lost his place in the development of this important railway. He had also promoted another line, certainly far less important, linking Canterbury and Whitstable. The engineering work was completed under the guidance of Robert Stephenson. It was an odd route with three hills along the way which were worked by stationary engines and cables – but one section was level and was worked by a steam locomotive, *Invicta*. The line opened on 3 May 1830 and can claim the distinction of being the first steam railway in the world to run a regular passenger service on a line between two towns. It had pipped the mighty Liverpool & Manchester to the honour, which had its grand opening in September of the same year. So where did passenger travel start? Was it with the Swansea & Mumbles, the Stockton & Darlington or perhaps the modest Canterbury & Whitstable? All had parts to play in the story, but it was the Liverpool & Manchester that set important trends as the first intercity steam railway. We shall look at that line and what it meant for passenger travel in the next chapter.

Chapter 2

INTERCITY

The chapter title is not strictly historically accurate, since neither Liverpool nor Manchester were officially cities when the railway between them was open, but in terms of their wealth and importance they certainly should have been. It was this that made the line so important – that and its need to provide railway features that had never existed before that time.

From the first, the company had looked to passengers as an important source of revenue and they had to provide facilities for them, starting with the carriages that would carry them. The only existing carriages on rails had really just been the old stage coaches with different wheels. Now that they had powerful locomotives to do the work of haulage, they could be far more ambitious and an early decision was taken to have three classes of carriage, each offering different standards of comfort.

The starting point was the frame and its wheels on which the wooden carriage body would be built. The frame itself was more or less the same as that used for the freight wagons, with frames inside and outside the four wheels, fitted with laminate springs of the type already in use on road carriages. Parts of the frame were extended to act as buffers. Couplings were loose chains.

A view of carriages on the Liverpool & Manchester shortly after the opening. The third class open carriages seem curious contraptions and there is some doubt as to the accuracy of the artist's work, as the locomotive is shown with equal-sized wheels, which it did not have.

Another view of carriages on the L&MR. The main difference is the presence of a canopy over the third class carriages. The wheel arrangement of the first class carriages is now more accurately shown, with the tops of the wheels above the frame

No original carriages have survived, but looking at the contemporary illustrations it is obvious that the design of first class carriages was very much based on stage coach design – indeed, they look very like the result of an accident which resulted in three coaches colliding and ending up all stuck together. Inside they were comfortably upholstered and had quarter-light windows at each side of the compartment door. The basic design soon proved to have a few problems, which is hardly surprising as nothing of the sort had ever been built before. Two problems appeared that were literally linked together. The first came when trains started up and the chains holding the carriages were pulled taut with an unpleasant jerk. A more serious problem occurred when trains stopped in a hurry and the carriages crashed together, providing the passengers with some nasty jolts – and even in some cases leading to suing the company for damages. The solution introduced in 1836 was to change the buffers and couplings. It was the work of Henry Booth, the company's secretary, who was far more than a mere administrator. He was the man who suggested using a multi-tube boiler in the engine being prepared for the Rainhill Trials, an absolutely essential feature in ensuring the *Rocket*'s triumph. Now he came up with another brilliant idea – screw couplings. As the name suggests, the screw could be used to either bring the coaches together or move them apart for uncoupling. They came into use in 1836. The solid buffers were at first padded with horsehair to reduce the impact but were soon replaced by sprung buffers. Altogether the changes made for a much more comfortable ride.

Braking still remained a problem. The brakemen or guards were perched on top of the coaches at regular intervals, and received a signal from the driver by means of the whistle that they should apply the handbrake. Not every coach had brakes. The brakeman who had the worst job was on the front carriage, where he was likely to showered with hot cinders from time to time.

Originally, the wheels were placed below the divisions between the three compartments, but this gave a very short wheelbase and an often bumpy ride. The general view was that wheels should be large, but carriage frames should be as low as possible. The trouble with the theory was that to reconcile the two requirements, the wheel arches had to intrude into the carriage, so they were set beneath the seats. It was not an ideal compromise, and the arrangement was soon changed in other early railways. By the 1840s the London & Birmingham had developed a first-class coach with wheels below the carriage. This was to become normal in later developments as can be seen in the illustration here.

The first class carriages had three closed compartments, with padded seating facing each other. Not everyone who could afford first class, however, chose to use the facility. The company also supplied flatbed wagons onto which a personal carriage could be loaded and secured in place. Those who travelled this way had the advantage of double springs – those on the wagon and those of their own

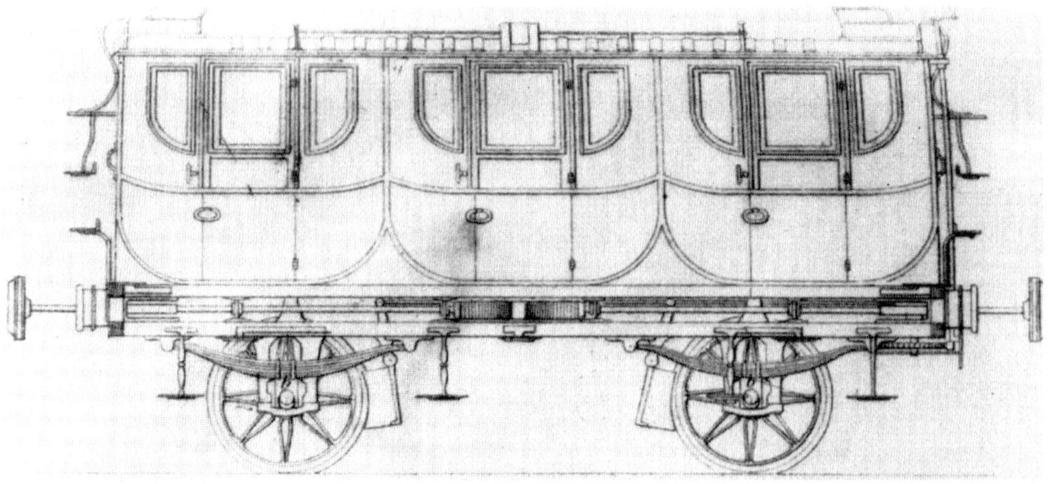

This London & Birmingham first class coach of the early 1840s is an improvement over the L&MR, with a wider wheel base and wheels below the frame. The illustration appeared in S.C. Breese, *Railway Practice* that appeared in five volumes between 1837 and 1847.

carriage. And, of course, there was no need to worry about who one might have to travel with if you were sharing one of the compartments – and as the early trains had no corridor, there was no escape from disagreeable company until the end of the journey.

There are two contemporary prints of trains, which differ significantly. In both, however, the carriages other than first class are more obviously based on goods wagons rather than stage coaches. In the first, the carriages have waist-high sides but are open topped and in these are the second class passengers, who seem to be very much crammed together on their plain benches. The third class appear to be basic wagons in which everyone is standing. In the second illustration, everything is much more orderly. Both sets of carriages are fitted with six rows of seats and a canopy, though the sides are still open. They do, however, come in two different forms, with one seeming to offer more protection from the elements then the other. Presumably these are again two different classes. Many companies followed these same basic designs, though some decided that the third class did not need any seating at all, which had the great advantage for the company that they could cram in far more paying customers. *The Railway Times* was quite firm on the matter: 'We do not feel disposed to attach much weight to the argument in favour of third-class carriages with seats.'

In the days of stage coaches, passengers normally waited at named inns, but with the large numbers now expected to travel by train this was no longer an option. They needed far larger premises – they needed stations where they could buy tickets and wait for the train. The original Manchester terminus was on Liverpool Road. This was not where the company had hoped to site the station. They had wanted to set it in Salford, to avoid having to bridge the Irwell, but the Manchester authorities wanted it to be within their town, so a house was bought on Liverpool Road that would be used by the station superintendent. A new building was then added alongside. There were problems to overcome. In order to reach the site, the railway had to cross a bridge over Water Street, and as a result the tracks appeared above street level.

Liverpool Road station. A curious feature is the sundial above the entrance for first class passengers.

The new station buildings were in the fashionable Georgian style, with two entrances, one grand one at the centre of the building for first class passengers and a more modest one at the side for everyone else. It was all reminiscent of a gentleman's house of the period, with a magnificent front door for the family and a tradesmen's entrance round the side. Inside was the booking hall and two waiting rooms, one large and comfortable and the other smaller and more austere. From here a staircase led up to the simple wooden platform with a canopy that was used for departing passengers. The arrivals platform across the tracks had no facilities at first, though station buildings were also added later. The complex also included substantial warehouses. By 1844, the facilities had become hopelessly inadequate and by this time, more lines were reaching Manchester, so a second station had to be built and after that the new Victoria station then handled all the passenger traffic. Liverpool Road was retained as a goods station and the buildings have survived intact and are now part of the Manchester Science and Industry Museum.

At the Liverpool end of the line, the first station was built at Crown Street, and was approached from Edge Hill by an incline, up which trains were hauled by cable. This was less than satisfactory, and in 1833 the company bought a new site – a former cattle market at Lime Street. The second station was opened in 1836. If the company had felt cautious about the public reaction to this new form of transport and had built Liverpool Road in a style that was reassuringly domestic, there was none of that here. The station was given a very imposing façade in the fashionable classical style. It was meant to impress – and does. There was to be major rebuild in 1849, when it was given a new roof over the tracks that was at the time the largest iron-framed roof ever built. Some of the original façade has been retained, but behind it is a totally rebuilt area. The intermediate stations were originally little better than halts. Rainhill, for example, home of the famous locomotive trials, did not receive anything like a station with facilities other than platforms until the 1860s.

The first step for anyone wanting to travel the new railway was obtaining a ticket, which was not the simple procedure that it would later become. The system used had been developed for the stage coaches, where a passenger booked in at the inn. A form was completed giving details of the journey, such as the destination, whether the passenger was travelling on the inside or on the outside of the coach. One copy was kept by the booking clerk, the second went to the coach guard and the third was given to the passenger. This laborious process worked well enough when just a few people were booking in but was impossibly slow for the hundreds now wanting to board a train. A new system was introduced in 1832 on the Leicester & Swannington Railway. First class passengers still had the paper tickets, but third class had metal tokens. These had the name of the company engraved, the destination and a serial number. The passenger paid the fare, received his token and the serial number gave the order in which they were to board the train. At the destination, the token was handed in and returned to the start for reuse. The system was rapidly adopted by the other early lines and remained in use for several years. We shall be looking at how the modern ticketing system developed in Chapter 4.

Several privileged individuals were invited to travel on the Liverpool & Manchester before the official opening, one of

An example of a metal ticket for the Newcastle, North Shields and Tynemouth Railway that opened as far as North Shields in 1839, from an illustration in the *Railway Gazette*.

whom was Frances Kemble, better known as the successful actress Fanny Kemble. She was to join the locomotive with a single carriage at Liverpool, but no doubt the engineer in charge of the engine that day, George Stephenson himself, could not resist offering the famously beautiful young lady a chance to join him on the footplate, which she accepted. She wrote a long account of her experience to a friend, starting with the journey down the deep rock cutting at Olive Mount:

> You can't imagine how strange it seemed to be journeying on thus, without any visible cause of progress other than

> the magical machine, with the flying white breath and rhythmical unvarying pace, between these rocky walls, which are already clothed with moss, and fern, and grasses; and, when I reflect that these great masses of stone had been cut asunder to allow our passage thus far below the surface of the earth, I felt as if no fairy tale was ever half so wonderful as what I saw. Bridges were thrown from side to side across the top of these cliffs, and the people looking down upon us from them seemed like pigmies standing in the sky.

They later stopped for water, and Stephenson 'explained to me the whole construction of the steam-engine, and said he could soon make a famous engineer of me, which, considering the wonderful things he *has* achieved, I dare not say is impossible'. They then set off again:

> We … set off at its utmost speed, thirty-five miles an hour; swifter than a bird flies (for they tried the experiment with a snipe). You cannot conceive what that sensation of cutting the air was; the motion is as smooth as possible too. I could either have read or written; and, as it was, I stood up and with my bonnet off 'drank the air before me' … When I closed my eyes, this sensation of flying was quite delightful and strange beyond description; yet strange as it was, I had a perfect sense of security and not the slightest fear.

Not everyone who was offered an excursion was equally enthralled by the experience. This account of 1829 is by the politician Thomas Creevey:

> Today we have had a *lark* of a very high order. Lady Wilton sent over yesterday from Knowsley to say that the Loco Motive machine was to be upon the railway at such a place at 12 o'clock for the Knowsley party to ride in if they liked, and inviting this house to be of the party. So of course were at our post in 3 carriages and some horsemen at the hour appointed. I had the satisfaction, for I can't call it *pleasure* of taking a trip of five miles in it, which we did in just a quarter of an hour – that is, twenty miles an hour.

> As accuracy upon this subject was my great object, I held my watch in my hand at starting, and all the time; as it had a second hand I could not be deceived; and so it turned out there was not the difference of a second between the coachee and myself. But observe, during those given miles, the machine was occasionally made to go it; and then we went at the rate of 23 miles an hour, and just with the same ease as to motion or absence of friction as the other reduced pace. But the quickest motion is to me *frightful* it is really flying, and it is impossible to divest yourself of the notion of instant death to all upon the least accident happening. It gave me a headache which has not left me yet … The smoke is very inconsiderable indeed, but sparks of fire are abroad in some quantity: one burnt Miss Ross's cheek, another a hole in Lady Maria's silk pelisse, and a third a hole in someone else's gown. Altogether I am extremely glad to have seen this miracle, and to have travelled in it. Had I thought worse of it than I do, I should have had the curiosity to try it; but having done so, I am quite satisfied with my *first* achievement being my *last*.

Henry Crabb Robinson was a journalist working for *The Times* but he changed his profession in 1809 and became a lawyer. He is best known as a diarist, and this entry for 9 June 1833 gives a clearer picture than most what it was like to travel from Liverpool on the Liverpool & Manchester in the early days:

> At twelve I got upon an omnibus, and was driven up a steep hill to the place where the steam-carriages start. We travelled in the second class of carriages. There were five carriages linked together, in each of which were placed open seats for the traveller, four and four facing each other; but not all were full; and, besides, there was a close carriage, and also a machine for baggage. The fare was four shillings for the thirty-one miles. Everything went on so rapidly, that I had scarcely the power of observation … Not quite a perfect level is preserved. On setting out there is a slight jolt from the chain catching each carriage, but, once in motion, we proceeded as smoothly as possible.

> For a minute or two the pace is gentle, and is constantly varying. The machine produces little smoke or steam … I should have observed before that the most remarkable movements of the journey are those in which trains pass each other. The rapidity is such that there is no recognising the features of a traveller. On several occasions, the noise of the passing engine was like the whizzing of a rocket. Guards are stationed on the road, holding flags, giving notice to the drivers when to stop,

The absence of smoke was due to the fact that on these early trains they were forced to use coke instead of coal as a fuel. One of the essential features of *Rocket* and the locomotives that came after it was the use of forced blast to increase the heat of the fire. Exhaust steam, instead of being allowed to escape into the air, was passed through a blast pipe at the base of the chimney, causing air to be dragged across the firebox. Sometimes, the effect was so fierce that embers were also pulled out and shot from the chimney in a shower of sparks. For one unfortunate passenger what could have been an annoyance became a disaster.

We are moving forward in time, but little had changed since the early days. The wealthy were still able to travel in their own coaches and embers were still flying. The Countess of Zetland was travelling to London from Darlington with her maid. The carriage was on a flat truck in the middle of the train.

> Soon after leaving Leicester I thought I smelt something burning and told my maid to look out of the window on her side to see if anything was on fire. She let down the window, and so many lumps of red-hot coal or coke were showering down that she put it up again immediately. I still thought I smelt something burning; she put down the window again and exclaimed that the carriage was on fire. We then put down the side-windows and waved our handkerchiefs, screaming 'fire' as loud as we could. No one took any notice of us. I then pulled up the windows, lest the current of air through the carriage should cause the fire to burn more rapidly into the carriage, and determined to sit in as

> long as possible. After some time, seeing that no assistance was likely to be offered us, my maid became terrified, and without telling me her intention, opened the door, let down the step, and scrambled out onto the truck. I followed her, but having unluckily let myself down towards the back of the carriage, which was on fire, was obliged to put up the step and close the door as well as I could to enable me to pass to the front part of the carriage, furthest from the fire, and where my maid was standing. We clung on to the front springs of the carriage, screaming 'fire' incessantly and waving our handkerchiefs. We passed several policemen on the road, none of whom took any notice of us. No guard appeared. A gentleman in the carriage behind saw us, but could render no assistance. My maid seemed in an agony of terror, and I saw her sit down on the side of the truck, and gather her cloak tightly about her. I think I told her to hold fast to the carriage. I turned away for a moment to wave my handkerchief, and when I looked round again my poor maid was gone. The train went on, the fire of course increasing, and the wind blowing it towards me. A man (a passenger) crept along the ledge of the railway carriages and came as near as possible to the truck on which I stood, but it was impossible for him to help me. At last the train stopped at Rugby station. An engine was sent back to find my maid. She was found on the road and taken to Leicester hospital, where she now lies in almost hopeless state; her skull fractured; three of her fingers have been amputated. I am told the train was going at 50 miles an hour.

This was an extraordinary accident, particularly as no officials seem to have been aware that anything was seriously amiss. Efforts to help were made by passengers, but they had no means of communicating with the footplate crew to alert them to the danger. The majority of accidents, however, came about simply because trains were such a novelty that passengers were not really aware just how fast trains were running. The most famous example came on the actual opening day. Eight locomotives were being used that day and the orders of the day made it clear that passengers should not attempt to leave their carriages when the train stopped to take on water at Parkhead. Among the dignitaries were the Duke of Wellington and the local MP William Huskisson, who had been an enthusiastic supporter of the railway. In spite of the warning about staying safe in the coaches, several passengers wandered about, crossing over the tracks. Huskisson, seeing the Duke's coach, walked over to speak to him. Then there were shouts of 'Get in, get in' as *Rocket* was approaching at speed. Huskisson seemed confused and clung onto the Duke's carriage door. The engine hit the door, hurling him onto the track, where the train rolled over one of his legs. He was rushed to hospital but died shortly afterwards.

W.M. Acworth in book, *The Railways of England*, 1889 listed the many bizarre ways in which people met their deaths, simply from a lack of understanding of the power and speed of locomotives. It would be almost comic if the results had not actually been fatal.

> Again and again it is recorded, 'injured, jumped out after his hat', 'fell off, riding on the side of a waggon'; 'skull broken, riding on top of the carriage, came in collision with a bridge'; 'guard's head struck against a bridge, attempting to remove a passenger who had improperly seated himself outside'; 'fell out of a third-class carriage while pushing and jostling with a friend'. 'Of the serious accidents reported to the Board of Trade,' writes one authority, 'twenty-two happened to persons who jumped off when the carriages were going at speed, generally after their hats, and five persons were run over when lying either drunk or asleep upon the line.'

Most passengers who travelled the Liverpool & Manchester, whether they found the experience delightful or frightening, agreed that the journey itself was smooth. One exception was a young engineer, who thought the ride was too rough and was sure he could improve on the way in which railways were built. His name was Isambard Kingdom Brunel, and we shall be looking at his solution in the next chapter.

Chapter 3

THE NETWORK SPREADS

The success of the Liverpool & Manchester saw an immediate wave of new railway proposals, not just in Britain but in many other countries as well. One of the most ambitious of the new schemes was for the Great Western Railway, to link Bristol and London. Brunel was appointed the chief engineer and now he had the chance to put his own ideas on railway construction into practice. George Stephenson had never seriously considered what would be the ideal gauge for a railway: he simply took the gauge for the old tramway for which he had built his first locomotive *Blucher* and continued using the same gauge for all subsequent lines – though somehow the original 4ft 8in gauge gained an extra half inch along the way. Brunel, however, felt that was inadequate, and he settled for a broad gauge of 7ft. He then decided that what he thought was a rough ride was due to the way in which the rails were set on sleepers and his track was to have the sleepers placed longitudinally, the full length of the track instead of spaced out at right angles to the rails. The sleepers were held together by metal ties, creating a rigid framework. As, apart from a short length of demonstration track at the Didcot Railway Centre, no trains have run on the Brunel broad gauge for more than a hundred years, we cannot know what the ride was like. Engineers have, however, shown that it was unlikely to be an improvement – rails need to have a certain amount of give. The broad gauge did, however, have one advantage in that their first class coaches, being wider, could accommodate eight passengers into each compartment instead of six and they had four of them instead of the three of the Liverpool & Manchester. So if there were 100 first class travellers, the GWR only needed three coaches, while the L & MR required six – less clanking at stopping and starting, so in that sense a more comfortable ride.

The greatest engineering work on the line was the Box Tunnel, nearly two miles long and built with a slight slope. This led one well known scientist Dr Dionysus Lardner to warn the public that if the engine failed, the whole train would gather speed, hurtle down the tunnel and reach a speed of a 100mph – a speed that no human being could survive. When the warning reached Brunel, he simply pointed out that there was a factor that learned gentleman had failed to take into account – air resistance. However, this dire warning was enough to alarm many passengers, who opted to leave the train and take a horse-drawn coach over the hill and rejoin the train at the far end of the tunnel. It took a while before it became obvious even to the most nervous traveller that nothing disastrous was likely to happen.

One enthusiast for the new railway was Queen Victoria, who wrote to the Belgian king from Buckingham Palace in June 1842: 'We arrived here yesterday morning, having come by the railway from Windsor, in half an hour, free from dust and crowd and heat, and I am quite charmed with it.' But according to a report in the *Morning Post* of the same year, her consort was less enthusiastic. 'Prince Albert invariably accompanies the Queen, but patronises the Great Western generally when compelled to come up from Windsor alone. The Prince, however, has been known to say, "Not quite so fast next time, Mr. Conductor, if you please."'

The royal couple would have had to go to Slough to catch the train, but could have gone to a station much nearer to Windsor had it not been for the Master of Eton. Brunel's original plan was to have a station there, but the Master objected on the grounds that pupils could catch the train and be tempted by the fleshpots of London. He insisted that if the railway was to come anywhere near the school, it should be shielded from view by a high wall stretching for four miles that the railway company would pay for. Eton has never had a station.

The GWR was at the time the longest railway route in the country, and with a journey time of around 4 hours, there was a rather obvious need for a stop in those days when toilet facilities on trains were non-existent. Swindon was roughly half way, so it was ordained that there would be a compulsory ten minute stop there. A refreshment room was opened that was let out to a caterer. It all looked very grand and had a coffee urn in the form of a locomotive. The coffee it produced, however, was apparently less than perfect. The owners were deeply offended by Brunel's criticism of their product and wrote to the engineer to complain, producing a famous reply from the engineer:

> I assure you Mr. Player was wrong in supposing that I thought you purchased inferior coffee. I thought I said to him that I was surprised that you should buy such bad roasted corn. I did not believe you had such a thing as coffee in the place. I am certain I never tasted any. I have long since ceased to make complaints at Swindon. I avoid taking anything there when I can help it.

Complaints about railway buffets rumbled on down the years.

Brunel's line was seen in isolation, but as the system spread throughout the country, a problem appeared. The other main lines all adopted the Stephenson gauge. Eventually the two systems were bound to meet head on. A famous trouble spot was Gloucester where the GWR met the Birmingham & Gloucester. Everyone had to change trains, which in itself is scarcely a problem. I live in Stroud on what was the GWR, and if I want to go Birmingham, I still have to change trains. But in the nineteenth century it was far more of a problem: everything had to be changed – one can imagine the chaos when a train full of passengers travelling north met another train heading south and everyone had to move between the two with all their bags and luggage. There was even more of a problem with freight trains. Something had to give, and it was the broad gauge that eventually had to be abandoned.

The spread of railways was not universally welcomed, and especially when they impinged on some of the country's most scenic areas. Not surprisingly, William Wordsworth was horrified at the idea of steam engines appearing anywhere near his home at Rydal, and wrote to Gladstone to complain. The most biting criticism, however, came from the writer John Ruskin:

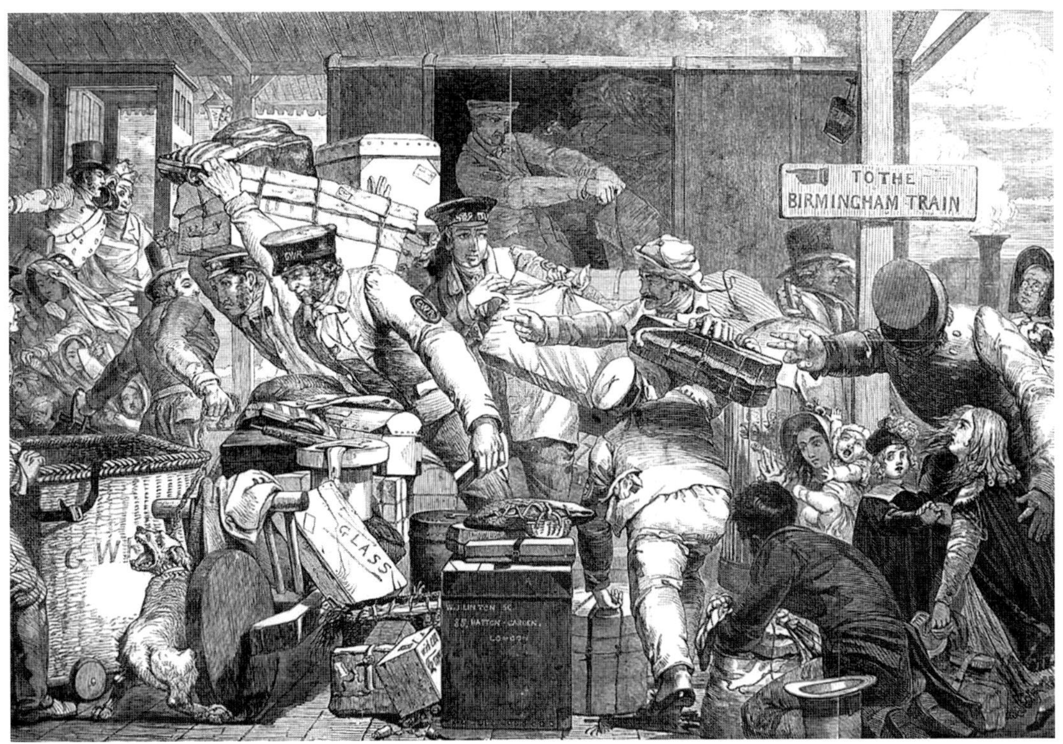

A cartoonist's view of the mayhem caused by the break of gauge at Reading station. It is doubtful if the scene was ever quite this chaotic.

> There was a rocky valley between Buxton and Bakewell, once upon a time, divine as the Vale of Tempe: you might have seen the gods there morning and evening – Apollo and all the sweet Muses of the light – walking in fair process on the lawns of it, and to and from among the pinnacles of the crags. You cared neither for Gods nor grass, but for cash (which you did not know the way to get); you thought you would get it by what *The Times* calls 'Railroad Enterprise'. You Enterprised a Railroad through the valley, you blasted its rocks away, heaped thousands of tons of shale into its lovely stream. The valley is gone, and the Gods with it; and now, every fool in Buxton can be at Bakewell in half an hour, and every fool in Bakewell at Buxton; which you think a lucrative process of exchange – you Fools everywhere.

Ruskin might be pleased to know that the line is no more, and what was once the track bed of the railway is now a popular route for walkers – the Monsal Trail.

The early railways of continental Europe had rolling stock that was often very little different from that of Britain, with similar carriages, ranging from comparatively comfortable for first class to downright uncomfortable for third. This is not too surprising, since in many cases the railway companies had gone to George Stephenson for advice and had bought engines and carriages from British companies. The first locomotive to operate on the Nuremberg-Fürt Railway in 1833 was supplied from the Stephenson works and the replica carriages in the photo on this page show an obvious likeness to London & Midland Railway stock. It is doubtful, however, if British footplate staff were ever quite this smart. Stephenson's importance is recognised by a carved inscription on the Italian station of Poggibonsi in the province of Siena: 'A la gloria imperitura di Giorgio Stephenson I ferrovarii di Poggi Bonzi' – to the glory of George Stephenson the railways of Poggibonsi.

Railways in North America had a rather bizarre start. A canal was planned to join Pittsburgh to Pennsylvania and work began in 1825. There was, however, a problem – in

The pioneering German locomotive *Der Adler* (The Eagle) built at the Stephenson works at Newcastle: the carriages are very similar to those used on the first British lines.

between the two cities were the Alleghenies, hills that rose to over 2,000 feet. The engineers, James Geddes and Nathan Roberts, came up with a unique solution. There would be two sections of canal, out from the two cities to the foot of the Alleghenies. Inclined planes, powered by steam, rose to the upper level, and there would then be a central section of 26½ miles laid with railway track. Special boats were built that could be split in two, hauled up the inclines and then used as carriages for the railroad. It was, however, still being worked by horses, not locomotives.

It was another canal, the Delaware & Hudson, that saw the introduction of locomotives. By 1828, over 100 miles of canal had been completed, that included a unique suspension aqueduct across the Delaware. The next 15 miles from the aqueduct to the Pennsylvania coalfield was to be covered by a railroad, and at this point it was decided to send one of the company's engineers, Horatio Allen, to Britain to buy locomotives, preferably from Robert Stephenson . In the event, he only ordered one from Newcastle; the other three came from Foster, Rastrick of Stourbridge. First to arrive was the *Stourbridge Lion,* but the trials were disastrous. Allen himself took the job of driving the engine, announcing that if there was to be any danger, then he would be the one to face it. The engine set off but left in its wake twisted rails and a badly damaged bridge. The engine never ran again. A much lighter locomotive, *Best Friend of Charleston,* with a vertical boiler was Allen's own design. Once again, he tried it out himself, but shortly afterwards the boiler exploded, killing the fireman. It was not the most promising start to the railway age in America.

The Baltimore & Ohio Railroad was originally operated by horses: a drawing made at the time when the company were just beginning to experiment with locomotives.

There were other attempts to develop railroads, but the most important was the Baltimore & Ohio, which was incorporated in 1827. The main promoters were Evan and Phillip Thomas, one of whom had visited Britain to see the Stockton & Darlington, and the line was very much based on the same pattern – a public railway where it was intended to use a locomotive for freight and a horse-drawn carriage for passengers. The early passenger coach looks remarkably crude – a shed on wheels. A locomotive was ordered from Britain, but the ship sank before reaching America. This enabled a local engineer, Peter Cooper, to build the country's first home-manufactured locomotive. It was a light engine with a vertical boiler, named *Tom Thumb* and went into service in 1830. The company then set about building their own carriages, which were extraordinary double-decker vehicles, one of which is preserved in the Baltimore railway museum. The wheels are set inside the frame, while the lower coach, very much on stagecoach lines, is suspended above it, and above that is a second open section with a canopy for cover. It is basically a two-class carriage where, as on the stagecoaches, you pay extra for inside seating. Other early railroads had even more bizarre rolling stock. The Erie & Kalamazoo Railroad which ran from Toledo to the mouth of the Kalamazoo River at Lake Michigan was opened as a horse-drawn line, but the following year it got its first locomotive. The illustration

An undated photograph of the replica of the Baltimore & Ohio locomotive with a train of double-decker carriages. One of these very strange vehicles can now be seen in the Railway Museum at Baltimore.

(p.39) shows the engine pulling a single, small double-decker carriage looking like a small cottage. It was not the speediest train in the world, taking around three hours to cover the 33 mile track.

The success of the Baltimore & Ohio encouraged the Americans to look to their own resources rather than relying on overseas manufacturers. They developed carriages unlike those in use in Britain. The most striking difference was that instead of a coach with sperate compartments, they were open from end to end, with seats ranged on either side of a central gangway. Charles Dickens toured America in 1842 and described a railway journey from Boston to Lowell, Massachusetts, which he wrote was typical of American railways:

> There are no first and second class carriages as with us; but there is a gentleman's car and a ladies' car: the main distinction between which is that in the first, everybody smokes; and in the second nobody does. As a black man never travels with a white man, there is also a negro car; which is a great, blundering, clumsy chest, such as Gulliver put to sea in, from the kingdom of Brobdingnag. There is a great deal of jolting, a great deal of noise, a great deal of wall, not much window, a locomotive engine, a shriek and a bell.
>
> The cars are like shabby omnibuses, but larger: holding thirty, forty, fifty people. The seat instead of stretching from end to end, are placed crosswise. Each seat holds two persons. There is a long row of them at each side of the caravan, a narrow passage up the middle, and a door at both ends. In the centre of the carriage there is usually a stove, fed with charcoal or anthracite coal, which is for the most part, red-hot. It is insufferably close; and you see the hot air fluttering between yourself and any other object you may happen to look at, like the ghost of smoke.
>
> In the ladies' car, there are a great many gentlemen who have ladies with them. There are also a great many ladies who have nobody with them: for any lady may travel alone, from one end of the United States to the other, and be certain of the most courteous and considerate treatment everywhere. The conductor, or check-taker, or guard, or whatever he may be, wears no uniform. He walks up and

An engraving of an early American carriage, called 'The Modern Ship of the Plains'.

> down the car, and in and our of it, as his fancy dictates; leans against the door with his hands in his pockets and stares at you, if you chance to be a stranger, or enters into conversation with the passengers about him. A great many newspapers are pulled out, and a few of them are read.

After describing a typical conversation with one of the American passengers, Dickens later recorded his impressions of the journey itself, which was actually quite short, not much more than thirty miles. He found the scenery to be desolate – 'mile after mile of stunted trees'. The route was mainly on a single-track line. It was a reminder that this was still a developing country. Having driven the same route, it is hard to imagine that it was once this rough and unmade. He continued with more details of the railroad itself:

> The train calls at stations in the woods, where the wild impossibility of anyone having the smallest reason to get out, is only to be equalled by the apparently desperate hopelessness of there being anyone to get in. It rushes across the turnpike road, where there is no gate, no policeman, no signal: nothing

> but a rough wooden arch, on which is painted 'WHEN THE BELL RINGS, LOOK OUT FOR THE LOCOMOTIVE'.

The crude safety measures were apparently not entirely satisfactory. George Combe, an English visitor to America, wrote a book of his travels that included this account of a journey on the Western Railroad of Massachusetts in 1839:

> On October 29 we left Springfield and started for Worcester by the railroad, which had been opened since we travelled to Springfield a month ago. Yesterday a stray horse had its legs and head cut off on this railroad by the engine, and the night before a carter had left a cart with stones standing on the track, which a train loaded with merchandise ran into in the dark and been smashed to pieces. We hoped to be more fortunate and were so; but although we encountered no danger, our patience was sufficiently tried. About ten miles from Springfield we came to a dead stop and the whole train stood motionless for three hours, enlivened by occasional walks in the sunshine and a visit to a cake store, the whole stock of eatables of which was in time consumed, the price of them having risen from hour to hour in proportion to the demand.
>
> The cause of our detention was the non-arrival of the train from Worcester, which, from there being a single track of rails, could pass our train here and nowhere else. We had heard nothing of its fate and expected it to arrive every minute till four o'clock, when at last an express on horseback came up and announced that it had broken down but that it was now cleared of the rails and that we might advance.

There were more delays before they set off again from Worcester for Boston. Combe was not greatly impressed with the arrangements, when they set off again a ten at night:

> The car was seated for 56 passengers and contained at least 30. There were no apertures for ventilation and when night came on, the company insisted on shutting every window to keep out the cold. A few who, like us, preferred cool air to suffocation congregated at one end where we opened two windows for our relief.

Further north, Canada was quite slow in building up its rail system, partly because it had a comparatively small population and partly because there wasn't much money available for investment – and, of course, it had a mixed population as well, partly English speaking, partly French and a few others who had emigrated from Europe, who didn't aways agree on what was needed. There was, however, a good case for building, as most transport was by rivers that froze in winter and stayed frozen until spring. Rivers were also liable to wander across the countryside. There was a need to provide a link between New York and Montreal. The last part of the journey was from Lake Champlain close to the border, via the Richelieu River and the St. Lawrence, a distance of 90 miles by river. Yet the distance from Le Prairie on the Richelieu to St. Johns, opposite Montreal was only 14½ miles. The bill for the Champlain & St. Lawrence Railway was a masterpiece of the bureaucratic art with endless clauses covering every eventuality. One sentence was 1,453 words long – James Joyce would have been proud to own it. As with early American lines, the first locomotive *Dorchester* was imported from Britain from the Robert Stephenson factory and the lines were laid to the British gauge of 4ft 8½in. On the opening day in 1836, so many crowded onto the train at Le Prairie – it was estimated at over 300 – that *Dorchester* huffed and puffed but failed to move. Only the passengers in the first two carriages enjoyed Canada's first steam excursion. The rest of the carriages were unhitched and pulled by horses.

Canada's second railway was built in Nova Scotia very much in the pattern of the early British colliery lines and was actually called the Albion Mines Railway. Opened in 1839, the locomotive was sent over from Christopher Hackworth's locomotive works at Shildon, and was typical of his work. It had a return flue boiler, the flue itself, being u-shaped which meant that the footplate was at the chimney end. Although mainly meant for freight, it did run a passenger service, with a weird carriage that looked like a summer house on wheels.

Canadian development was not just slow, but amazingly so compared with many other regions. By 1850, Britain had 6,621 miles of track, but the United States had rushed ahead with 9,021. Canada could only manage a meagre 68 miles.

The first locomotive supplied to Nova Scotia was built at Timothy Hackworth's works at Shildon on the Stockton & Darlington Railway. The coach is crudely constructed, and there is little sign of any springing involved.

In spite of the advances made around the world, Canadian passengers seemed unprepared for the new experience. Progress on the St. Lawrence was halted at Montreal by the Lachine Rapids, that dropped the river by 46 feet. It had been bypassed by the Lachine Canal, and now it was decided to add a railway to link the navigable sections. The engineer in charge was a Scot, Alexander Miller, and at first the line was run using two American locomotives. But then, in 1847, a more powerful locomotive arrived from Scotland, an impressive machine with 6ft diameter drive wheels. Miller took the engine out on its first run himself and covered the 7½miles in 11 minutes, an average speed of around 45mph. Several terrified passengers went up to him and pleaded to go slower on the return journey: To pacify them, he agreed to slow down, but once he got on the footplate, he couldn't resist giving the new engine a real work out – the return took just 9 minutes!

These early lines were all built to the British standard, but there was a brief excursion, on a line joining Portland, Maine, to Montreal that was built to 5ft 6in and others followed for

To complete this set of rather odd carriages; the oddest of all must be this one of the Erie & Kalamazoo Railroad in Ohio, opened in 1932.

a time. But, as in Britain, the confusion of gauges was found to be uneconomic, and Canadian lines are now almost all at 4ft 8½in. The confusion was not limited, however, to Canada; a similar story can be told of developments in Australia. The first engineer to arrive to oversee railway construction was an Irishman, F.W. Shields, who had decided that his native country needed something more generous than the Stephenson gauge and settled for 5ft 3in and he persuaded the Australians that their vast country needed the same gauge rail. Then he had a disagreement with the Sydney government and resigned. His place was taken by a Scot, James Wallace, who was equally determined that the 4ft 8½in system should be employed and persuaded Sydney and South Wales to adopt it. Victoria and South Australia had already invested too much in the broader gauge to change. Just to make matters more complex, Queensland got round to building lines in the 1860s and cash was short, so they went for a narrow gauge of 3ft 6in. It probably seemed a good idea at the time.

Railways in Australia were in many ways very different from those in other parts of the world in that instead of joining existing settlements, they created them. The civil engineer

C.O. Burge who was involved was not impressed when he went to work in New South Wales. The first line he surveyed was supposed to be 'populous' but in the first thirty miles he only found 'one squatter'. He then had to find sites for towns. His view on the existing towns was scathing – 'the deadly, drab, dull similarity of one to the other I never saw equalled except in a sack of peas'. But the towns were built, and their existence was only made possible thanks to the railways.

By 1860, railways had been constructed all over Europe, were spreading rapidly in North America and work had begun in South America. India had its first lines and construction had begun in Egypt and South Africa. There were still many areas, however, especially in Asia, that were still to have any rails – China and Japan had to wait until the 1870s. But the spread of railways throughout the nineteenth century led to new challenges and new types of passenger services. We shall be looking at those in chapter 5.

The opening of Australia's first public steam railway at Melbourne in 1854.

Chapter 4

THE STATION

Railway stations mark the beginning and end of a journey. It might start from the familiar station of one's home town but arrive at somewhere the traveller has never visited before, and the station will be the first impression received. It might be the grand terminus in a city centre or a lonely country halt, but it will have its own characteristics.

As the rail network spread throughout Britain, so main line stations became ever grander. The first stations at Liverpool and Manchester had what were, in effect, two separate stations: one for arrivals, the other for departures. London's first main line terminus was the London & Birmingham's Euston station. Opened in 1837, the original was comparatively straightforward, differing from earlier stations in having a partially glazed roof over the tracks. It was designed by the architect Philip Hardwick, with a hint of classicism in the details, such as the supporting iron columns. A hint at classicism, however, was not enough.

> The entrance to the London Passenger Station opening immediately upon what will necessarily become the Grand Avenue for travelling between the Metropolis and the midland and northern parts of the kingdom, the Directors thought that it should receive some architectural embellishment. They adopted accordingly a design of Mr. Hardwick's for a grand but simple portico which they considered well adapted to the national character of the undertaking.

The Doric Arch as it came to be known was demolished in the 1960s when modernisation was going ahead and it was felt by the authorities that classical styles did not fit the new image. Many disagreed with what they saw as

The imposing entrance to Euston station photographed c.1900. It has since been demolished in the interests of modernisation.

an act of architectural vandalism. There was also a similar arch at the Curzon Street station in Birmingham. There the opposite scenario was played out. The arch remains but the station has gone. The site has now been chosen for a new station to serve the proposed HS2 line, and the plans call for the arch to be retained in the structure. Meanwhile Birmingham passengers use what must be Britain's dullest station – New Street.

When the Great Western Railway reached London, it was originally served by a modest station at Bishop's Bridge Road, while at the Bristol end of the line there was the altogether grander Temple Meads. As with the other main line stations, the latter looked back in time for its architectural inspiration – here it was right back to the Middle Ages with an imitation hammer beam roof. It did not remain in use as the main Bristol station. When the line was extended westward towards Cornwall, a new through station was needed. By 1854 a new London station had been opened at Paddington, then at the edge of the city. It was the joint work of engineer Brunel and architect Matthew Digby Wyatt and it made no concessions to architectural pastiche. There is no very grand façade – the station itself is in a cutting and the approach is down ramps on either side. It is only when the traveller reaches the station itself that its true glory is revealed, an astonishing building that has been called a cathedral of glass and iron. This was a thoroughly modern building of two great curved glazed roofs over the tracks, held on an iron framework. An article in the *Illustrated London News* written at the time of the opening neatly summed it up. 'The principle adopted by them was to avoid any recurrence of existing styles and to make the experiment of designing everything in accordance with the structural purpose of the nature of the materials employed.' It would have been a revelation to the first travellers who arrived here and it remains as imposing today. I have been living in the west of England for very many years, and Paddington has been my arrival point for visits to London, and I still get a thrill from this great station.

The construction of the Great Western produced a new problem for travellers, especially when it was extended right down to Penzance. People set their clocks and watches by the position of the sun at noon and that was their 12 o'clock. But noon at London comes about 20 minutes earlier than noon at Penzance. Trains run to a timetable and it is up to the crew on the train to keep to that timetable. But how do you do that if everyone along the route has a different time? The answer was to have timetables based on railway time, which was to be the same everywhere and based on London time. Stations were issued with clocks with an extra hand – one minute hand pointed to local time, the other to railway time. The original clock from Stroud station in Gloucestershire has been preserved and can be seen in the town library. America used a similar system in sorting the problem out before the country was officially divided into time zones. It was based on local time in the principal cities along the route. Not everyone approved. T.S. Hudson travelled across America in the !880s:

> We left Washington for the West in the forenoon, taking parlor-car tickets for Cumberland and sleeper tickets to Cincinnati for night traveling. A great source of inconvenience in traveling is what appears to be the foolish arrangement of clocks. An attempt is made by every large place to use solar time, hence trains are made to run as nearly as possible to the time of the sun. In the 40 hours' ride now commenced, we had three times – Washington, Vincennes and St. Louis. It became indispensable to carry with our watches, a reconciliation card with little dials showing the hour at a dozen different places when noon at New York.

The iron and glass over roof for the train shed became a feature of many major stations around the world, but the largest was over the train shed of the Pennsylvania Railroad

The Pennsylvania Railroad's Jersey City station with its immense train shed, and steam ferries from New York lined up outside from *King's Handbook of New York City* 1892.

PENNSYLVANIA RAILROAD. JERSEY-CITY STATION.
FERRIES TO DESBROSSES STREET AND TO CORTLANDT STREET, NEW YORK.

Kingoonya station on the Trans-Australian Railway served a settlement of around 200 families in the 1930s. The township is now largely deserted.

station at Jersey City, with a massive span of 306ft. It was part of a larger transport system, linking in directly to ferry services to New York. Different companies in different cities around the world had their own ideas how to provide a suitably imposing sight for visitors. The São Bento station, Porto reserves its finest work for the interior, where the concourse is covered in exquisite tiles depicting historic scenes. But few can compete for architectural splendour and a certain idiosyncrasy with the Chhatrapati Shivaji terminus (formerly Victoria terminus) Mumbai, with its exotic mixture of European Gothic and Indian Moghul architecture. One later station of note was the Central Station in Milan, officially opened in 1931. By then, Mussolini was in power, and the building reflects in its very typical Roman architectural façade, the desire to create a new Italian empire to match that of the past. But, of course, most railway stations around the world are not that grand. Thousands are simple basic structures, providing the basics of ticket office, platforms and waiting rooms and some did not even have the most basic facilities. Australia was a very sparsely populated country when the first railways were built, and some small settlements had to make do with unstaffed halts. Anyone wanting to catch a train had to hold up a signal for the driver, and anyone wanting to alight there had to warn the train staff in advance.

Journeys normally start with buying a ticket. The early ticket systems were unsatisfactory and cumbersome. A major improvement was made by Thomas Edmondson.

Hoping the train will stop; ladies holding out a signal at Woodford, a small rural town in Queensland. It is now home to a narrow gauge steam railway museum.

He was born in 1792 and began his working life as a grocer and cabinet maker, but in 1836 he was appointed as station master at Milton near Brampton in Cumbria on the line from Newcastle to Carlisle. It was a small station that left him time to think about tickets. He realised that it was not really necessary to laboriously write out the details of each passenger's name, so long as they had a valid ticket of some sort. However, there needed to be some way of ensuring that an unscrupulous clerk didn't just give out the ticket and pocket the money. His solution was a cardboard ticket which was stamped with a number and the type of ticket. He printed rows of tickets with consecutive numbers that could be stored in a specially constructed box with the lowest numbered ticket at the top. A mechanical system issued the tickets in order. He improved the system over the years and with his brothers formed the Edmondson Ticket Company to manufacture tickets, which the company still does today, though no longer relying on railway tickets. It was eventually recognised that a passenger might attempt to cheat the company by claiming only to have come to meet someone. The platform ticket, without which non travellers could not pass the ticket barrier was only introduced in the early twentieth century.

The spread of the railways created a new problem. A long journey could involve a passenger crossing over tracks owned by a number of different companies, each of whom would want paying for the privilege. But how was this to be organised if one ticket covered the whole journey? The answer was the Railway Clearing House, established in January !842 at an office near Euston Station. This was set up originally to serve the London & Birmingham, Midland Counties, Birmingham & Derby Junction, North Midland, Hull & Selby,

Clerks at work at the Railway Clearing House in the 1930s.

Manchester & Leeds, Leeds & Selby, York & North Midland and Great North of England Railways. Later the scheme was expanded as more companies joined in. To ensure that everyone paid up, the Clearing House was given the right to sue by an Act of Parliament of 1850. From a modest start, it became a massive institution with a large clerical staff. Each month, the tickets collected at the end of a journey were sent in from the different companies, the proportion of the fare allocated to each company was sorted out and payments arranged. The station ticket collector was an essential part of the whole process.

The cardboard ticket became the norm on railways everywhere, with variations. In America, 'coupon tickets' were introduced, with each section of the coupon being removed as the train passed from one system to the next. Collecting the tickets was the job of the conductor on the train. Not everyone understood the system, and a senator from the Pacific coast taking a train to the east was one of them, as told in an anecdote by Horace Porter, Vice President of the Pullman Palace-Car Company. The senator was suspicious of anyone who came from the east and when the conductor asked to see his ticket, he refused at first. Then he relented as far as letting the official see it, but when the conductor tore off the first section, he was incensed and punched the man. When passengers intervened, the agitated senator gave this explanation. 'Why', said the Senator, 'I paid 17 dollars and a half for a ticket to take me through to Cincinnati and before we're five miles out, that fellow slips up and says he wants to see it, and when I get it out, he grabs hold of it and goes tearing it up right before my eyes.'

Once inside the station, passengers waiting for the train had a variety of options, depending on the size of the station. Most would have waiting rooms, often with separate rooms for men and women and the larger stations might have refreshment rooms. A new facility appeared in 1841, when William Marshall opened a bookstall on Fenchurch Street station on the London & Blackwall Railway. The idea was soon taken up by William Henry Smith whose first bookstall was opened at Euston in 1848, selling newspapers and cheap books, and soon W.H. Smith stalls were spreading throughout the network. Individual railway companies began producing their own books for sale in the form of guides to what could be seen of interest along the routes. In some cases, the books were arranged so that one page had the view as seen from one side of the carriage and the facing page showed the view from the other. The best-known guides of all, however, were the Bradshaws. George Bradshaw produced his first railway timetable – *Bradshaw's Railway Time Tables and Assistant to Railway Travelling* – in 1839, a modest book costing just twopence halfpenny. Later editions soon got bigger and started to include details about places along the routes and a book that in 1845 had just 32 pages had grown by the end of the century to a massive 946 pages. The Bradshaw guides were no longer limited to describing British rail journeys but were describing European routes as well and later even further afield. The equally famous Baedeker guide books were not specifically designed for railway travel.

The book stall at Paddington c.1910. As well as offering books and newspapers, the stall is festooned with GWR advertisements for rail excursions.

Arrival at a station was not the same in every country, as Frederick S. Williams discovered and he described his French experiences in his book of 1852, *Our Iron Roads*:

> Continental railways have peculiarities unknown in this country, which appear very strange, and are sometimes rather annoying, to Mr. Bull when he crosses the Channel. In England, the traveller goes to the station when he pleases, lounges in the waiting-room, consumes Banbury cakes, and drinks scalding coffee ad libitum, wanders about the platform, and superintends his own luggage, and, in fact, so long as he does not interfere with the convenience of other people and does not violate the 'bye-laws' of the Company, he can do what he likes without let or hindrance. In France, the system is very different: instead of the traveller managing himself, he is managed. On procuring his ticket, he delivers up his luggage, pays a sou or two, and obtains a receipt, and is then marched into a waiting-room, according to the class of his fare; as if the Company were afraid that, having paid his money, he should not have his ride. When the train is ready, the first-class passengers are liberated, and every one scrambles to his seat, with as much agility as circumstances will admit; the second-class travellers follow; and the third-class are then allowed to deposit themselves in the vehicles prepared for their reception. The second-class carriages have the advantage of being lined with ticking, and are quite as comfortable as the old stage-coaches used to be in this country; but the speed of the trains is only about twenty miles an hour.

One rather surprising fact, which certainly would have seemed odd to an English traveller, was that the station staff all carried swords. Williams does, however, end by admitting that the French facilities are generally much better than the British. French station restaurants provided far better food – it is difficult to imagine any self-respecting Frenchman even attempting to eat at the Swindon dining room.

Rail travellers often required accommodation at or close to the station, either because they had an early train to catch or were arriving late at night. Several companies in Britain provided their own station hotels, of which the best known is at St. Pancras. The Midland commissioned the leading architect of the day to design a 300-bedroom hotel. The building was inspired by the Gothic revival and even had such medieval features as gargoyles on the façade. The interior was no less exotic, featuring an immense double staircase. Other companies built their own hotels but nothing on this grand a scale. Having the hotel right next to the station, virtually part of the structure, had its advantages in that the passenger got straight off the train and straight into the building. However, as I discovered when spending a night in the Crewe station hotel, it can have one disadvantage: one keeps being woken up by station announcements from the nearby platforms. Around the world, however, entrepreneurs saw the advantage of building hotels as close as possible to the station.

In the nineteenth century, stations had more staff than they have today, mainly because they had far more jobs to do. Many passengers expected to have porters to carry their luggage and all kinds of goods had to be loaded into and taken out of the luggage van. As well as staff for the ticket office, there always had to be a ticket collector to meet each arriving train, and at many stations there was also an adjoining goods yard or goods shed that had to be

Often mistaken for being part of the actual station, the resplendent former Midland Hotel, St. Pancras has recently been restored to its full Gothic glory.

The station hotel at Martinsburg West Virginia, the multi-storey building to the left was originally built for the Baltimore & Ohio Railroad in the 1840s.

manned. One important part of the job was dealing with the early morning milk train, carrying heavy churns for local delivery. The staff under the station master were responsible for ensuring that everything was in order before the guard on the train could give the signal to move off and there were the general duties of keeping stations in good order. Originally, boards carrying information on train arrivals and departures had all to be set by hand. For the passengers, however, the main contact was with the baggage porters, who they were expected to tip for their services. Many years ago, as a student, I took a summer job as a temporary porter on Harrogate station and learned a valuable lesson in life. I thought the head porter was being generous when he showed me where the first-class compartment would be stopping. A rather haughty lady summoned me to take her large and heavy pieces of luggage to the taxi rank and off I staggered to be rewarded by a sixpence tip. My 'helpful' porter carried one light case for a lady from third class and got a shilling. I was surprised, until he explained why

Station staff at an unnamed South Eastern Railway station in the early twentieth century

the experienced porters avoided first class: 'Folk like them didn't get rich by giving it to folk like us.'

A surprisingly large number of stations throughout the world remain much as they were when first built though the facilities they offer may have changed. Journeys still require tickets, though they may have been purchased online rather than from the ticket office and the chances of getting anyone to carry suitcases are negligible in many places. But the carriage that the passenger gets into has changed greatly since the earliest days.

Chapter 5

CARRIAGE DEVELOPMENT IN THE NINETEENTH CENTURY

The early carriages, based very much on the old stage coaches, slowly gave way to more distinctive railway carriages, the curved lines giving way to straight lines and flat surfaces, although flat roofs soon gave way to elliptically-curved roofs. Poorer passengers, however, still had to make do with open carriages and, in the case of the Great Western, these were frequently attached to slow goods trains. Change came not because the railway companies felt their passengers deserved better treatment but as the result of a fatal accident. It was Christmas Eve 1842 when a goods train left Paddington at 4.30 in the morning with two open third class carriages attached between the wagons and the locomotive. Unknown to anyone, heavy rainfall had caused a landslip in the deep Sonning cutting and in the darkness the train ran straight into it at full speed. The carriages and wagons were all loose-coupled and as a result the impact sent the wagons crashing forward, crushing the carriages against the tender. Eight men were killed and seventeen seriously injured. The matter was brought up in parliament, largely because the men had actually been working on the construction of the new Houses of Parliament. A Board of Trade enquiry was set up and resulted in what became known as the Gladstone Act of 1844 that ordered all railway companies to provide at least one train each weekday in both directions, stopping at every station along the route. It would have to include third class compartments with seats and protection from the weather. The trains had to travel at not less than 12mph and fares were set at one penny per mile. They became known as parliamentary trains.

The companies were not notably enthusiastic about the Act, worried that if they provided decent and cheap travel for third class passengers, it might tempt those who would have been prepared to pay for second class to switch to the cheaper option. One solution took advantage in a certain vagueness in the wording. They were required to run two trains a day – but no one had specified the times, so they offered cheap fares in the new carriages at decidedly unsociable hours – late at night or very early in the morning. The situation was summed up in *Lloyds Weekly Newspaper* in 1952, reporting that the trains were 'as uncomfortable as the law would allow', started at 'the least convenient hours' and moved at a speed 'that wearies out all patience'.

The Midland took a different approach from the rest, providing a decent fully enclosed coach with three compartments, glazed windows and oil lamps in the roof. They also began attaching the new coaches to their fast trains. This horrified the other companies and also had a knock-on effect. If third class passengers were getting coaches comparable to those available to those paying for second class, and travelling on the same trains, then the latter wanted something more for their money. Improvements were made, including upholstering the seats in second class. The Eastern Counties started using coaches with both first and second class in the same vehicle. They were still the fairly basic structure, carried on four wheels with just three compartments. The centre compartment was first class, with windows in both doors and well upholstered seats with head rests. The second class compartments were narrower, with just one window, rather less plush furnishings and no head rest. Eventually, as the distinctions between third and second class travel narrowed down, most companies limited themselves to just two classes but, because the regulations still required the parliamentary trains to be run, it was the second class that was eliminated. This explains the curious arrangement that dominated British rail travel of having just first and third class compartments.

The development of coaches was comparatively slow, with for a long time four wheels being the norm, with

The Eastern Counties Railway was among the first to introduce comfortable second class accommodation, as here in this composite carriage of the 1840s.

the exception of the Great Western, who soon brought in six-wheeled coaches. Some of the Great Western coaches were subdivided longitudinally with just four travellers per compartment. Lighting was by oil lamp fitted into the divider, so the light was shared out between four sections. Following the Gladstone Act, even third class carriages were provided with lighting, but usually just one small lamp for the whole carriage. This was possible simply because they were seldom divided into sections but were open throughout with bench seats or they only had very low partitions. Even in daylight, they were gloomy as they were often provided with few windows and those they did have were generally small. In the open coaches, there was only a door at the end.

One feature of the early trains was the guard perched high above a carriage, operating a hand brake. It was a less than ideal arrangement – especially for the guard, exposed to the weather and sometimes showers of hot cinders. The earliest solution was the brake coach, where an end compartment was for the sole use of the guard. In some he had a special, glazed extension above the level of the roof from which he could keep a look out. It became known as a birdcage. An alternative was to have an extension projecting from the side of the guard's compartment, known as a ducket, though the origin of that name is obscure. One place where one can see variations on these early developments is the Isle of Man Railway, opened in 1870, that still uses its nineteenth century rolling stock that includes four-wheeled carriages with no corridors and coaches with ducket guard's compartment with a hand brake. By the end of the century, guards' vans in Britain were separate vehicles that were also used for luggage.

In general, coaches in Britain were still constructed entirely of wood on a wooden frame, though in some cases the underframe would be strengthened by metal strapping. Their appearance, however, was greatly improved by the care taken over their paintwork. Everything was done by hand, including in most cases elaborate lining out, lettering for the doors, often in an ornate style and even company crests. Coat after coat was added – the Midland were said to have used no fewer than seventeen to provide a high gloss finish. But if the outside looked grand, the degree of comfort to be had inside was distinctly limited. There was no heating in the early days, which seems barbarous to us, but was probably more acceptable to the first railway travellers. Their previous traffic experiences were limited to travel in unheated stage coaches and not everyone even got to ride inside. Dr William

A South Eastern Railway brake coach of the 1850s: the 'bird cage' look out for the guard raised above the level of the roof.

The Isle of Man Railway has retained much of its original rolling stock, including this brake coach, with its protruding side window for the guard.

Kitchiner in his book *The Travellers' Oracle* of 1827 gave this advice: 'If circumstances compel you to ride on the outside of a Coach, put on Two Shirts and Two Pairs of stockings, turn up the collar on your Great Coat and tie an handkerchief around it, and have plenty of dry Straw to set your feet on'. Whether they followed the good doctor's advice or not, two passengers on the London to Bath coach in the winter of 1812 were found to have frozen to death when the coach arrived at Chippenham. Travelling even in a chilly railway carriage was at least an improvement on that, and many railway companies offered to hire out blankets and foot warmers for the journey. A major improvement came in 1874 when the Midland introduced a heating system based on a stove and hot water pipes and gas lighting for the carriages. The gas was supplied from a reservoir, usually set beneath a carriage.

As journeys became longer, other facilities started to be needed. The London & Birmingham introduced the first

primitive form of sleeping accommodation in 1837. The coach itself was in effect a standard first class carriage but was converted into a sleeper by means of a stretcher-like contraption consisting of two bamboo poles, joined by webbing, covered with cushioning. This was laid across the facing seats, but as the compartment was comparatively narrow, passengers' feet were stuck into a hollowed out portion, known as 'the boot'. The demand for sleeping cars was not pressing, where distances travelled were seldom very great. It was a very different case in America.

A nineteenth century gas-lit coach. The gas is contained in the cylinder beneath the carriage.

The American railroad network had been steadily expanding, but mainly in the east. In 1854, tracks were opened from Chicago to Rock Island, Illinois on the Mississippi. *The Rock Island Line* became a popular song, but its significance is in the name. The rock island itself was in the middle of the river, which made it the perfect place for a pier for bridge construction. The idea was strenuously opposed by the owners of river boats, who feared the competition. Nevertheless, the bridge was built and opened for traffic on 22 April 1856 and was considered a great triumph but was to prove a short-lived one. On 6 May, a packet boat from New Orleans crashed into a pier and started a fire that rapidly spread through the whole wooden structure. Suspicion that this was deliberate was heightened when the next boat up the river was displaying a banner with the message: 'Mississippi River Bridge Destroyed. Let All Rejoice'. Nevertheless, the lines continued to be pushed eastward, eventually reaching St Joseph, Missouri. Meanwhile, on the other side of the country, a line had been completed from San Francisco to the state capital Sacramento. Work started on the first transcontinental from both ends – the Central Pacific from the west, the Union Pacific from the east.

The story of the transcontinental railroad of America has been the subject of many a dramatic movie, usually involving battles with the Native Americans. In reality, the Native Americans seem to have done little more than mount occasional raids, not to stop the 'advance of the iron horse' but to pillage the stores. One such foray was seen off by a contingent of US Cavalry, after which the officer in charge declared he'd never have any more problems with the Sioux. That turned out to be a notably inaccurate forecast, for the young officer was George Custer, eventually promoted to General and he was to meet his death fighting the Sioux at the Battle of Little Bighorn. The real railroad battle was between the workers of the two railroad companies, as the companies received land grants depending on how far they managed to push their lines. The Central Pacific had the harder task, having to force their way through the Sierras, a task that involved a vast amount of tunnelling. There were so many tunnels, in fact, that the company developed special cab-forward locomotives so that the footplate staff would not be constantly enveloped in smoke. The Union Pacific had the flat prairie land for their route. The two met at Promontory Point, Utah on10 May 1869 and America had finally been crossed by rails.

The transcontinental railway was a triumph, but the trains showed little improvement from earlier times; the wooden coach was still the norm and on the whole was very basic. A feature was the veranda at the end from which passengers mounted and dismounted. Away from the main cities, American trains often stopped at the new settlements that were still being developed and which had only minimum facilities as they were seldom served by more than one or two trains a day. Platforms were usually of wood and quite low, so mounting blocks had to be placed to allow people to get on and off. Much of the traffic consisted of the immigrants, who had once had to make their way west in the famous wagon trains, but who could now travel by rail. The British author Robert Louis Stevenson, best known as the author of *Treasure Island,* followed emigrants from Britain and joined them on the west bound Union Pacific. He has left a detailed account of the journey in his book *Across the Plains* (1892) that is worth quoting at length:

> I suppose the reader has some notion of an American railroad-car, that long, narrow wooden box, like a flat-roofed Noah's Ark, with a stove and a convenience at either end, a passage down the middle, and transverse benches upon either hand. Those determined for emigrants on the Union Pacific are only remarkable for their extreme plainness, nothing but wood entering in any part of their constitution, and for the usual inefficiency of the lamps, which often went out and shed but a dying glimmer even while they burned. The benches are too short for anything but a young child. Where there is scare elbow-room for two to sit, there will not be space enough to lie. Hence the company, or rather as it appears from certain bills about the Transfer Station, the company's servants, have conceived a plan for the better accommodation of the travellers. They prevail on every two to chum together. To each of the chums they sell a board and three square cushions stuffed with straw, and covered with thin cotton. The benches can be made to face each other in pairs; and the chums lie down side by side upon the cushions with the head to the conductor's van and the feet to the engine.

Stevenson paid $2.50 for this less than luxurious arrangement. Meals on the long journey were also a problem:

> Before the sun was up the stove would be brightly burning; at the first station the natives would come on board with milk and eggs and coffee cakes; and soon from end to end the car would be filled with little parties breakfasting upon the bed boards. It was the pleasantest hour of the day.

> There were meals to be had, however, by the wayside: a breakfast in the morning, a dinner somewhere between eleven and two, and supper from five to eight or nine at night. We had rarely less than twenty minutes for each; and if we had not spent another twenty minutes waiting for some express upon a side track among the miles of desert, we might have taken an hour to each repast and arrived at San Francisco up to time.

At Ogden in Utah, he changed to the Central Pacific:

> The change was doubly welcome, for first we had better cars on the new line, and second, those in which we had been carried for more than ninety hours had begun to smell abominably… The cars on the Central Pacific were nearly twice as high, and so proportionately airier, they were freshly varnished, which gave us all a sense of cleanliness as though we had bathed; the seats drew out and joined in the centre, so that there was no need for bed boards, and there was an upper tier of berths which could be closed by day and opened by night.

There were, of course, other trains offering better facilities for those who could afford to pay more than poor emigrants. While Stevenson was travelling with emigrants, the more affluent enjoyed a very different experience. Already by the 1880s the wooden cars intended for the wealthier travellers were given exotic interiors, more like Victorian parlours than traditional railway carriages, with colourful upholstery, patterned carpets, curtains at the windows and on some even stained glass windows at the ends. Parlour cars were even more luxurious, places where passengers could sit in considerable comfort, and in the case of ones reserved for men, smoke and drink. The biggest change, however, had come somewhat earlier.

In the 1850s, young George Mortimer Pullman and his bride left by train on their honeymoon, and he was not impressed by the experience. He was convinced there was a market for a better service and tried to convince various companies to take up his idea, but with no success. He decided to set up in

The completion of the railroad across America, when the Union Pacific and Central Pacific joined resulted in long journey times. The carriages were luxuriously appointed, and the one shown here was fitted with a harmonium for Sunday services.

business for himself and bought a conventional coach from the Chicago & Alton Railroad. He made it into a parlour car that could be converted into a sleeping car at night. Altogether twelve of these vehicles were built, but they were not a success. Development was brought to a halt by the outbreak of the Civil War in 1861, but the war turned out well for Pullman. He made a great deal of money trading with gold mines in Colorado and when the war ended in 1865, he used his funds to design an entirely new coach. The coachwork was still wooden, but on an iron frame and instead of wheels on fixed axles, the carriage was mounted on two four-wheeled bogies with springs and rubber shock absorbers. The interior was fitted out in splendour with comfortable chairs that could be converted into beds and overhead berths that folded down at night. He named it the *Pioneer*.

The design was sound, but the companies shied away from running the heavy vehicle over their tracks. It seemed Pullman was facing failure again, but once again he benefitted from a tragedy. In 1865, Abraham Lincoln was assassinated and his body was to be taken from Washington for burial at his birthplace in Illinois. Pullman suggested that the *Pioneer* coach was suitably dignified, and his offer was accepted. Now railroad companies who had claimed the car was too heavy for their tracks had no choice – they could not refuse to carry the funeral train. Crowds lined the track to pay their respects to the former President and had a chance to see and marvel at the Pullman coach. It was a publicity coup and established the coaches as a new standard of luxury and smooth running. Pullman went on to design 'hotel cars' that

A rather crude book illustration showing one of the original Pullman cars.

served as both dining cars and sleepers. Once again, the beds were neatly stowed away during the day, and passengers sat at tables where the food was served.

The interior of a Pullman first class car from the first decade of the twentieth century. It is shown ready for day use, with the beds tucked away above the seats – the curtains can be seen that provide privacy at night time.

The success of the Pullman cars was not limited to America. In 1874, the Midland Railway began importing prefabricated Pullman cars, which were then assembled in Britain. They remained special throughout the steam age and passengers paid a premium to use them. They were unlike other British coaches of the period in being open instead of being divided into compartments and having just a single door. In the 1950s, during my brief spell as a porter, the arrival of the Yorkshire Pullman was an event, but led to an embarrassing experience. It was not uncommon for porters to help load luggage onto the racks in the compartments of other carriages. I was asked to do the same for an elderly lady on the Pullman. But with just the one entrance, by the time I had fought my way past everyone else to the middle of the carriage, the door had closed, the whistle had blown and I was off and spent most of the rest of the day making my way back to Harrogate station.

The success of the Pullman trains encouraged the other British railway companies to consider offering better facilities, including dining cars. There was, however, little point in having a dining car unless passengers could reach it. The result was the development at the end of the nineteenth century of the side corridor carriage. The corridor ran the length of the carriage and was connected via flexible junctions to other carriages, so that passengers could walk the whole length of the train. It had the disadvantage that it reduced the size of the passenger compartments, but that was more than compensated for by the increased sizes of the carriages themselves. There was one other advantage to the side corridor carriages; all passengers now had access to a toilet. The first train toilets were not exactly hygienic as the waste was simply dropped down onto the tracks – hence the sign requesting passengers not to use the facility in the station area. As schoolboys, who like most kids revelled in lavatory

A typical third smoking class compartment on a Great Western Railway corridor train at the start of the twentieth century.

humour, we used to sing this feature of trains to the tune of Dvorak's *Humoresque*. It began:

> Gentlemen will please refrain
> From passing water while the train
> Is standing in the station
> If you please.

The style of the corridor carriage compartment changed little in Britain for decades. Upholstered bench seats, windows on either side of the door and a third sash window in the door itself that could be raised and lowered by a leather strap. The luggage rack above the seats was a usually a string netting slung between iron brackets. Making the netting was one of the few jobs in a carriage works that went to women. Elsewhere, in the nineteenth century, very little had changed anywhere, with the bodywork still in the hands of traditional coach builders working with wood.

But bigger and heavier carriages presented their own problems. Braking could no longer depend on a simple hand brake operated by the guard. Braking on locomotives had already been improved with a steam powered system. The brake blocks were held back from the wheels in the off position by springs, but steam could be admitted to a cylinder and the power used by a mechanical connection to the piston to overcome the spring resistance and move the brake block. This was efficient but there was no way of applying it to the rest of the train by passing the steam down pipes to the carriages – it would simply condense before it became effective. The solution was found by the American inventor George Westinghouse. He realised that you could make a connection throughout the train if you used compressed air instead of steam. Individual air brakes on the carriages would all come into operation at the same time. As an extra precaution, there was a cock in the guard's van that could be opened to operate the system in an emergency. He introduced his air brake in 1869 and improved it two years later – it became the new standard braking system, greatly improved train safety and made it possible to build bigger and better carriages.

Pullman carriages appeared in many different countries, and were always well received, but few thought to thank the company in verse. In 1875 Pullman established a workshop in Turin and a Mr A. Rapp was sent from America to supervise construction, and the workers presented him with these lines when the work was finished:

Welcome, welcome Master Pullman
The great inventor of the Saloon Carriages,
Italy will be thankful to the man
For now and ever, for ages and ages.

To Master Rapp we men are thankful.
Cause of his kindness and adviser sages
Our hearts of true gladness is full;
And we shall remember him for ages.

It is not perhaps great poetry nor is the English immaculate, but would an English workforce fare any better if they tried to write poetry in Italian?

So far, all the travel we've been looking at has involved the use of steam locomotives, but a new form of traction was given a try in the 1840s. This was the atmospheric railway, in which air was pumped out from one end of a tube, allowing air pressure to push a piston along. If a train could be attached to the piston, then it would be pulled along. There was an early attempt in what was known as Mr. Clegg's Pneumatic Railway of 1840. This was improved by two brothers, Jacob and Joseph Samuda. They laid a 1½ mile track with a 9in diameter pipe with a slit in the top, through which a flange emerged to which a vehicle could be attached. To keep the pipe airtight, it was covered by leather flaps reinforced with iron that could be pushed aside as the piston moved down the tube and would close again after it had passed. The first railway to use the system was the Dublin & Kingstown on their branch line between Kingston and Dalkley. The flange itself was attached to a small truck to which carriages were linked. There was an unexpected demonstration of its power when Frank Ebrington was sat on the truck, waiting for the carriages to be attached. Before that could happen, the

A very basic third class carriage on the Sultan's Railway, Syria in 1908.

system was started up and he shot down the track at the unprecedented speed of 80 miles an hour.

A far more ambitious scheme to use the system was the work of Isambard Brunel, who decided to use it for the new railway that would link Exeter to Plymouth. The first test run was made in February 1847, and after a few early problems had been sorted out, a full service was initiated between Exeter and Newton Abbot. The local press greeted it with enthusiasm. 'The novelty of the thing begins to disappear: passengers go in and out with the same indifference they would manifest towards a stage coach. Master Piston is getting a general favourite. Indeed many prefer its noiseless track to the long drawn out sighs of "Puffing Billy".'

But problems appeared in winter, when the leather froze on some days and the whole track became unusable. The leather itself soon began to deteriorate and it became obvious that the whole system would need constant and expensive repairs, with all the hold ups to traffic that would involve. The system was abandoned, but the passengers who did use it at least experienced a novel form of railway transport.

The British were not alone in building atmospheric railways. In France, a new railway linking Paris to Saint Germain-en-Laye was begun in the 1830s but never got beyond Le Pecq, where the next section was considered too steep to be worked by locomotives. However, the Inspector General for French railways, M. Mallet, investigated the Irish system and decided that it would be just the thing to overcome the problem. A 1.5 km line was built in 1847, with two steam engines to evacuate the tube and the trains were able to conquer the 1 in

A carriage on the atmospheric railway section of the line from Paris to St. Germain-en-Laye.

28 incline at the very respectable speed of 35 km/hr. The train ran back under gravity. Unlike the English line, this French line was very successful and remained in use right up to 1860, when more powerful locomotives became available.

Standards offered to passengers varied throughout the world in the nineteenth century. In India, for example, many carriages did away with glazed windows altogether and simply had openings with protective bars – not so much an economy measure as a way to keep the compartments cool in the absence of any form of air conditioning. In northern countries the problem was less one of keeping cool in summer than getting warm in winter. Steam heating through flexible couplings to radiators in the compartments was first introduced to Great Western side corridor trains in 1892. Looking at the stock in use in different countries, one finds a huge range, from the very basic to the luxurious. But by the start of the twentieth century, travel by train had become far more comfortable than it had been at the beginning of the railway age for passengers in every class of coach. And for a select few, there were new luxuries to be enjoyed on special trains.

On Indian railways, in order to keep them cool, many of the carriages had unglazed windows with protective bars.

Chapter 6

TRAVELLING IN LUXURY

Among the first people to enjoy genuine luxury on a train journey were Queen Victoria and Prince Albert. The queen had several coaches built over the years, the best known of which was built at the London & North Western works at Wolverton in 1869 and is now part of the National Collection housed at York. This was a double unit, consisting of a day coach and accommodation for her personal servant, and a night coach with a bedroom and a compartment for her dressers. Originally this was in two separate sections, but they were later combined as a single carriage on two six-wheeled bogies. As one might expect, everything in the day coach was on the grandest scale, with richly upholstered furniture, a great deal of gilding and was originally lit by candles and oil lamps. Although electric lights were installed at a later date,

Queen Victoria's saloon of 1869, which is now preserved in the National Railway Museum in York

the queen apparently never turned them on. She was assured a peaceful night, as the bedroom floor was lined with cork and the sides and the walls and ceiling were padded with quilting to deaden the noise. She also had another set of carriages kept for her across the Channel for when she travelled in Europe.

Grand as they were, they looked almost plain compared with the carriage built for Maximillian II of Bavaria in 1864 and now housed in the Nuremberg Transport Museum. The exterior with its gilded swags gives at least a hint of the baroque extravagance of the interior. It must have suited Maximilian's successor, Ludwig II, who became famous all over Europe for his taste for extravagant architecture – an obsession that earned him the nickname 'Mad Ludwig'. Other nineteenth century monarchs also displayed their grandeur when they travelled by rail, as did the Maharajahs of India – a fine example is the Mysore Maharajah's preserved in the Delhi Railway Museum. One of the last of the old-style gilded set of royal coaches was built for Umberto II of Italy in 1929 by Fiat. The three coach set is preserved at the National Railway Museum in Pietrarsa. Styles of royal saloons changed with the times, and the one built for Elizabeth II might be less ornate than that supplied to Victoria but looks a good deal more comfortable. Private carriages were available on some lines, particularly in America and one company based in New York had a successful business hiring them out.

There were many who were not grand enough to have a private car specially built for them or did not require an entire car on hire. But if they were wealthy enough to pay for extra comforts, when and if they became available, then the luxury trains were the answer. Such trains first became available in the nineteenth century thanks to a young Belgian, Georges Nagelmackers, whose banking family had been heavily involved in financing railway development in their country. When he was 21 years old, he set about wooing a cousin, but when he was rejected, he decided to travel, whether to provide a distraction from his damaged pride or simply from a wish to see the world is not known, but in 1869 he arrived in America. Given the family background, he was interested in new railway developments and was particularly impressed by the Pullman cars. He spent a year in the country and although he was impressed by the Pullmans, he was not sure that the more class-conscious Europeans would welcome the open carriages. He did, however, see a future for a new generation of trains in Europe, but not perhaps as radical as the American prototypes. At the end of the year, he was back in Belgium, keen to put his ideas into practice.

In April 1870, a brochure appeared promoting the idea that Nagelmackers et Cie were to provide sleeping cars for the continent, and at the head of the list of subscribers was the name of King Leopold II. The next stage was to design the sleeping cars. Outwardly, they had nothing new to offer, simple carriages on six wheels and not fitted with the new air brakes. Inside they were very different from the Pullmans, having a side corridor and separate compartments, each fitted with comfortable chairs that folded down at night to make into beds and upper berths. There was a single toilet compartment at the end of the coach. The original vehicles were ordered from an Austrian firm and later from the Rathgeber Works in Germany. They were intended for a route to link Paris to Berlin. The timing could hardly have been worse – the year operations were due to start saw the outbreak of the Franco-Prussian war. There was a hasty change of plans, and the cars were rerouted to run from Ostend to the Italian port of Brindisi.

All seemed to be going well, but at the end of the war, the Cenis tunnel was opened, passing through the Alps and offering a new, short route from France into Italy. Nagelmackers responded by forming a new company, La Compagnie Internationale des Wagons-Lits and acquired a new partner, Colonel William Mann, an American who had fought under Custer in the American Civil War. He proposed going beyond the sleeping-car to providing 'boudoir cars' just as Pullman had done. Together they formed the Mann Boudoir Sleeping Car Company and, much as Pullman had done, looked to get publicity – Mann supplied a special car for the great beauty of the day Lily Langtry and then another to take the Prince of Wales to St. Petersburg. As Nagelmackers set about promoting routes through Europe, he found that Mann had a somewhat unsavoury reputation and, as a man of scrupulous honour himself, he decided to end the partnership

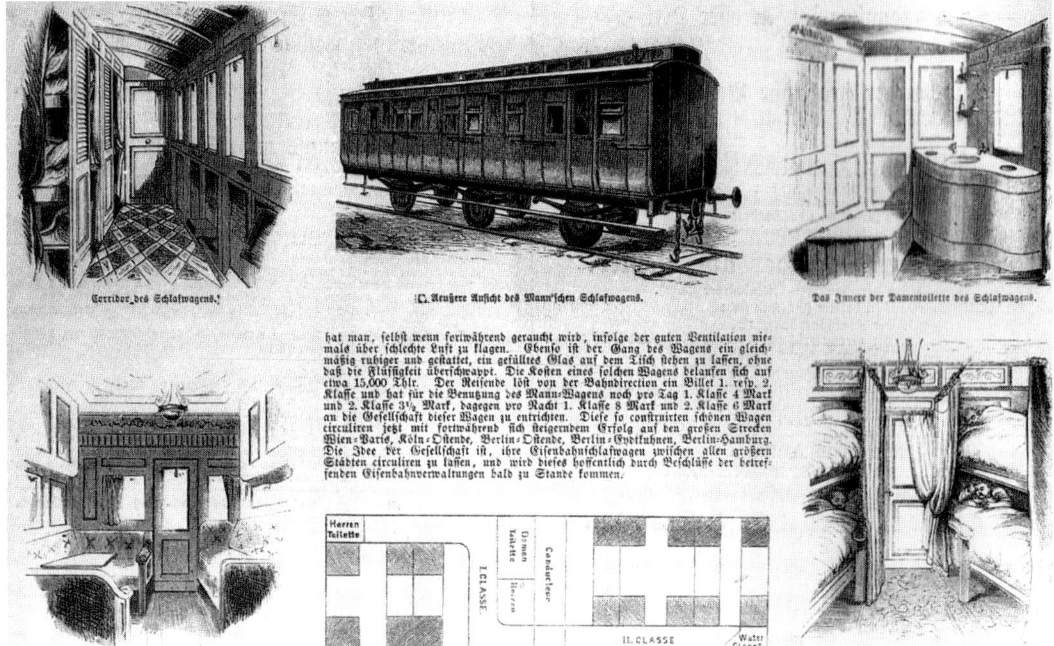

A set of illustrations showing the layout and different compartments of the Mann Boudoir Car of 1874, with compartments made up for day and night use.

by buying up the American's share – and the Comapgnie Internationale des Wagons-Lits was reborn in 1876.

Nagelmackers now began the tortuous business of obtaining running rights through different European countries, linking Paris to Berlin, Rome and Calais for the cross-Channel trade. In 1882 he introduced his first dining car to run between Marseilles and Nice as a trial. It had a central kitchen and two saloons, one for ladies and gentlemen and a smoking saloon for men only. It was a success, and he was now able to achieve his ultimate ambition. He had acquired running rights through from Paris via Strasbourg, Salzburg, Munich, Vienna, Budapest and Bucharest to Constantinople (Istanbul today). On 4 October 1883, the Gare de l'Est in Paris was to see the departure of the first of these trains that now had an exotic name. It was the Orient Express. The crowd who had turned up to see this new phenomenon were disappointed when they saw one of the old Mann boudoir cars at the platform. This was a little piece of theatre devised by Nagelmackers – for the real Orient Express had yet to appear. Then, one of the latest 2-4-0 express locomotives with imposing 1.5 metre driving wheels steamed into the station hauling a rake of imposing coaches in a shining royal blue livery. Immediately behind the tender was a *fourgon* or baggage car that carried mail bags – an important source of revenue. Then came two sleeping cars and a dining car with a second *fourgon* bringing up the rear.

The new carriages were very similar to Pullmans, mounted on two four-wheeled bogies. The interiors of the wagons-lits were resplendent. Each carriage held twenty passengers in compartments fitted out with leather embossed chairs and panelled in teak, mahogany and marquetry. At night, the beds were made up with silk sheets and each carriage had two toilets, with an attendant who nipped in after each user to ensure perfect cleanliness. The dining car was even grander, with the restaurant itself flanked by a smoking room for men and a boudoir for the ladies. Two French journalists had been invited along and they were not going to be impressed by the décor if the meals were not up to standard. Happily, Georges Boyer of *Le Figaro* was more than delighted by the meal and described the chef as a genius. The menu was varied to reflect the area through which they passed and was accompanied by appropriate wines of the region. It was served by white-gloved waiters – a vote of confidence in the steadiness of the ride. All the staff wore smart uniforms with gold braid and were all under the control of the chef de train, who made sure every traveller was happy.

The journey itself proved quite eventful. At Szeged in Hungary, they were greeted by a band who played for them on the platform and then joined the train and gave a vigorous performance of *La Marseillaise* with singing led by the Burgundian chef. At Bucharest, the passengers were

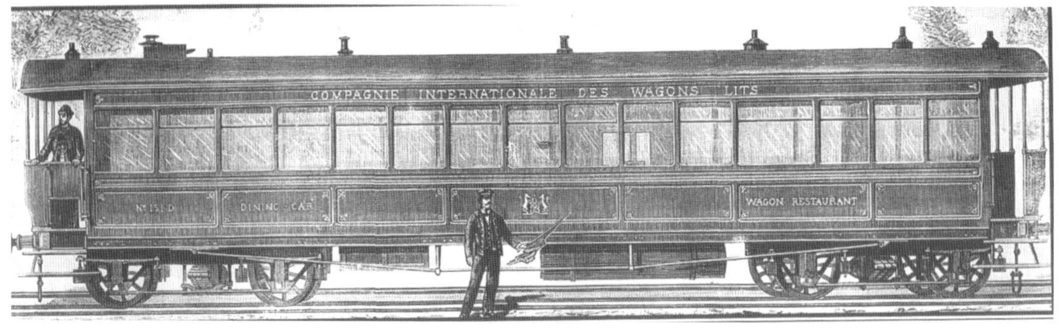

Car 151 D used as part of the train for the inaugural run of the Orient Express, which, with its bogie wheels provided a much smoother run than the earlier Mann Boudoir Car.

An Orient Express dining car from the early twentieth century, when the décor was at its most elaborate.

invited to visit the exotic mock-medieval Pele Palace built for King Carol of Rumania, where they would be greeted by the monarch himself. The gentlemen were concerned about not having formal dress but were assured that the king understood that was the case. The excursion was not a success. The king had decided they would enjoy the walk to the palace, but soon after they set off it poured with rain, and they were greeted by King Carol in full dress uniform, which embarrassed the visitors.

The biggest disappointment came when they reached the Danube for the crossing into Bulgaria – but no bridge. They had to join a ferry and continue on their way via a train with none of the grandeur of the wagon-lits and that only took them to the Black Sea, from where they finally made their way to Constantinople by steamer. There was time for sightseeing before they were ready for the return journey, eventually arriving back in Paris on 13 October. It was generally agreed that the whole trip had been a success, in spite of the few problems. The Orient Express was established as the ultimate luxury train, an honour that it was to retain for decades to come.

Alternative routes were found to improve the service to Constantinople. There was only one dark day in the build up to the better service and that came on 3 May 1891. The train was passing through Eastern Thrace when the driver realised that the track had been sabotaged. With no time to stop the engine, he and the fireman leapt off the footplate. The engine plunged down an embankment, carrying the two local coaches behind the tender with it, but the link to the wagons-lit snapped leaving them upright on the track. A band of men appeared armed with guns and knives, led by a burly Greek, Anasthatos, who reassured the passengers that they were not bandits but freedom fighters and that no one would be harmed – a fact that did not stop them stripping the cars of everything of value, though they graciously returned items of sentimental value such as wedding rings. They took hostages – five German bankers and the engine driver, who were released after a ransom of £8,000 was paid and in a final quixotic gesture, Anasthatos gave each of the hostages five gold sovereigns, which might not have impressed the bankers but would certainly have pleased the engine driver. There was criticism of the company for routeing the train through notorious bandit country. Fortunately, however, the Orient Express was rerouted following the completion of a bridge over the Danube in 1894, when the journey was then continued to the port of Constanta, where there was a good steamer service. The attack on the train was, however, just the first event that was to give the Orient Express a reputation for mystery and intrigue in fact and fiction.

There were a series of bizarre events on the famous train and many strange passengers. Among the latter was Sir Basil Zaharoff, a gentleman who appears to have started his professional life as a pimp in Constantinople but went on to make a fortune in dubious arms deals. In January 1866, the Duke of Marchena boarded the train with his 18-year old bride, Maria Berente. No one had warned the young woman that her husband was mentally ill. Zaharoff heard screams in the corridor, opened his compartment door to find Maria in a blood-stained nightdress, screaming that her husband was trying to kill her, a story that was rapidly confirmed when the knife-wielding Duke appeared in the corridor. He was disarmed and the grateful Maria became Zaharoff's mistress. When the Duke died in 1924, they married and had their honeymoon inevitably on the Orient Express.

Constantinople may have been an attractive destination in many ways, but it was also at the heart of a very troubled region. There was a large Armenian population in Turkey, but at the end of the nineteenth century the Turkish authorities branded them all as potential terrorists. Among the Armenians was Calouste Gulbenkian, who was extremely wealthy but felt that for the sake of his family they had to escape. They dressed in their oldest, shabbiest clothes, he with a bundled-up carpet under his arm, his wife with a bundle on her head. In spite of their shabby appearance as, it seemed, poor carpet sellers, they were welcomed on board the famous train. Only then was it revealed that the wife's bundle contained all the family's gold and jewellery and inside the carpet was their infant son. Gulbenkian in later years used the train many times, without the need for disguise, and it was said that there were houses at every stop where a girl waited for the multimillionaire to call.

Travelling through so any different countries, the Orient Express soon had a reputation as the favourite means of travel for international spies. The most famous of these was a Dutch woman, Margaretha Zelle, better known by her stage name, Mata Hari. She made her reputation as an exotic dancer in Paris, when she offered to do 'traditional Javanese Dances' – an offer that received little interest until she explained that this involved dancing in the nude. She became a star of the Folies Bergères. She was a regular traveller across Europe. Her many lovers included both the head of German Intelligence and the French Minister of War, a combination that led to her arrest in 1917 and execution as a spy. Another dancer at the Folies had an equally dramatic story, though the beginning was entertaining not tragic. The Afro-American dancer Josephine Baker called for one of the attendants vey late at night, long after even the express's kitchen had closed down, and asked for a drink and a sandwich. He explained that everything was closed: she offered to do her famous banana dance for him. As her costume for the dance consisted of nothing more than a very short skirt made of a string of bananas, it is not perhaps surprising to hear that she got her snack. She was to be involved in another incident on the train on 12 September 1931. The far-right Arrow Cross League was responsible for setting a bomb on the track on the Biatobargy viaduct just outside Budapest. The locomotive and ten cars fell into the ravine: twenty people died instantly, many more were injured and shocked. Josephine Baker was among the uninjured passengers so to help calm everyone down she gave an impromptu performance of her best known cabaret songs, including her hymn to Paris, *J'ai deux amours*.

The years after the First World War saw big changes with a great increase of cross-European connections, and the formation of the Simplon-Orient Express. The name recognised the importance of the Simplon tunnel through the Alps, taking trains through France and Switzerland to Milan and onwards to Venice and Trieste, together with new connections through the new country of Yugoslavia to Constanta and a branch to Athens. Milan was also the starting point for an express service to Bordeaux, with trains made up almost entirely of wagons-lits. To meet the extra traffic, Milan acquired a new station, the biggest in the world covering 42 hectares. It is a curious amalgam. The main entrance, concourse and booking hall were all grandiloquent in the more ornate Victorian fashion, but behind the train shed was uncompromisingly modern. The coaches for the Orient Express also took on a new look. New steel bodies were added and by the 1930s the interiors had lost their fussiness and been remodelled in the new fashionable art-deco style. They included marquetry and decorative glass panels by Lalique. Some of these magnificent carriages are still in use. The new Venice-Simplon Orient Express begins at London Victoria with a journey in Pullman carriages to Folkestone, where passengers leave the train for a scheduled service through the Channel tunnel. It is at Calais that they join the new train with the historic coaches. It is a mark of the sheer romance of the old Orient Express that passengers are prepared to pay considerable sums of money for what would otherwise be just another, if rather long, rail journey.

Great Britain, being an island, was for some time isolated from the luxury trains of Europe. French trains were often

The immense train shed at the Milan Central station, opened in 1931.

given rather exotic names, and the one connecting Paris to Calais was known as the Flèche d'Or. In 1929, the British began a new service intended to link directly to the French and they simply translated the name; it was to be the Golden Arrow. The service was begun using all first class Pullman carriages, headed by the Southern Railway's latest express locomotives, the 4-6-0 Lord Nelson Class. One of the appealing features of the train was the fact that luggage was carried through from London to its final continental destination, without the traveller having to bother about it. A special long truck was attached at the rear of the train containing several large boxes for 'registered luggage'. These were fastened to the wagon by chains and would not have to be inspected by customs until they crossed the last frontier on their journey. So, if a passenger had booked through to Rome, they would be untouched until they reached the Italian frontier.

On reaching Dover, the passengers embarked on a specially commissioned first class only steamer, the *Canterbury*. The registered luggage boxes were loaded on board and unloaded at Calais and stowed on the luggage van of the Flèche d'Or.

A dining car on the Flèche d'Or, among its notable features are the decorative glass panels by the famous Lalique company.

The new train would usually contain a mixture of Pullman coaches and wagons-lits and would be headed by a 'Pacific' 4-6-2 locomotive. Some of the wagons-lits would later be detached and attached to the 'Blue Train' heading for the French Riviera. The usual departure time from London's Victoria station was 11 in the morning and the passengers would expect to arrive at the Gare du Nord in Paris at 5.40 pm. In later years, the Golden Arrow was forced to abandon its first class only status, when faced with competition from the new air services that became available, offering the wealthy an even quicker connection between the two capitals.

Luxury trains arrived in North America at quite an early date. The first was the Pennsylvania Railroad's Pennsylvania Limited service to Chicago that went into service in 1887. It used Pullman vestibule cars, the vestibule being a covered section at each end of the carriage that served two purposes, providing cover for passengers moving between carriages and acting as a buffer zone. Carriages were loose coupled and in the event of a sudden stop prevented the wooden carriage compartments from telescoping into each other. The cars were unmistakable – painted green below window level, yellow above and given red roofs, earning them the nickname 'the yellow kids'. Other companies had their own versions, such as the North Western Limited linking Chicago to Minneapolis. There was a certain amount of rivalry, not least in the quality of food served on board. The dining cars of the Santa Fe's California Limited carried a sign with the simple message 'It is the best in the world'. Among the offerings were tenderloin steak at 80 cents or baked trout for a modest 45 cents. Not everyone, however, was delighted with the fare they received on every line. A correspondent writing in the *Railway and Locomotive Engineering* magazine in 1904, for example, was less than delighted with his trip on the Pennsylvania Limited. The train itself was excellent, though he thought the carriages overheated, but he was not happy with the dining arrangements, that were controlled by the Pullman company:

> I want to say most emphatically the 'dollar a meal' system ought to be abolished. Who wants to eat a dollar breakfast? Then comes luncheon and dinner; I am quite willing to pay

> a dollar for dinner, but I am not willing to pay a dollar for each of these meals and be glared at by a waiter because, in his eyes, my tip is too small, and be given a finger bowl the water in which has been used by someone else.

The Pullman waiter was almost certainly on low wages and was relying on generous tips to make a living. For the return journey the dissatisfied diner took the Chicago, Milwaukee and St. Paul and his reaction was very different, describing it as the trip of a lifetime:

> The railroad is very smooth, the cars are the very finest, the attendants – conductors, porters, waiter and the men in charge of the dining cars – most kindly and attentive. The food is excellent, abundant, and carefully served: the 'tips' it suited me to give were accepted in a nice manner, the men seemed pleased.

To the north of the United States, Canada was developing its own rail system. The first sleeper car service opened on the Grand Trunk Railway between Montreal and Toronto in 1857. It was greeted with enthusiasm by a writer in the *Montreal Leader*:

> Perhaps in no respect has science achieved results conferring more comfort on the traveller than are to be found in the night cars of the Grand Trunk Railway. Literally we are embodying the dream of youth, when we read of Sinbad and of the Flying Horse. Who 20 years ago could have thought it possible that a party of Gentlemen would enter a comfortable saloon and after an hour's chat and a well-served supper each would take a rest upon a lounge and find himself next morning before breakfast 300 or 400 miles from whence he started, with untired energy and fit for exertion?

It was a start, but it was not until 1886 that a railway connection was completed across the whole country, when the Canadian Pacific opened its line from Montreal to Port Moody on the Pacific coast. The train was hardly one of all-out luxury as it covered virtually every class of passenger. There were two very basic sleepers for immigrants, one second class carriage, two first class, two sleepers and a dining car. The train left Montreal on 28 June and finally reached Port Moody on 4 July. Even today, anyone travelling the full width of the country from Halifax Nova Scotia to Vancouver by train will face a journey time of five days. Clearly, such a journey demands a certain degree of comfort and good facilities. Many years ago, I travelled around half of that distance from Halifax to Winnipeg, and as a young man only used to standards on British trains, it all seemed quite remarkably comfortable and well organised. It was not, however, it has to be said, the most scenic of journeys. Leaving Halifax, the view through the window seemed to be of interminable woodland and waking up the next morning, the view seemed to have changed not at all; even the trees looked the same. Later, when arriving in the Prairie region, there was even less to see apart from vast areas of land given over to growing grain. Other parts of the world certainly offered more visual excitement, but to be fair to Canada, I never managed to take the train through the far more magnificent scenery of the Rockies.

The best known luxury train in Africa is the Blue Train, but it has its origins in an earlier version, the Union Limited that came into service in 1923, running between Cape Town and Johannesburg. The train consisted of first class saloons, a dining car with a separate section to hold the kitchen and accommodation for staff and an observation car. The company certainly offered a wide range of facilities, including hot and cold showers as well as wash basins. At night, both upper and lower bunks had recessed electric lighting, the current provided by dynamos attached to the axles. The staff offered shoe cleaning and valeting services.

None of this is very different from the service offered by other luxury trains, but the Union Limited did have one very fundamental difference. Johannesburg stands at an elevation of 1,753 metres above sea level. To reach the city from Cape Town was going to involve finding a way up through the mountain passes. At first, the engineers constructing the first lines out of Cape Town built, as many others had done throughout the world, to the British standard gauge. It soon became apparent, however, that this was totally unsuitable for tackling the mountain passes directly, which was going to

The very well equipped kitchen on a Canadian train of the 1930s.

involve sharp curves. As a result, the line was built to a 3ft 6in gauge instead. The line had to cross the Hex River Mountains 120km from Cape Town that rise to a height of over 2,000m. The climb up to the Pass involves an average gradient of 1 in 40 and was only achieved by snaking up the hillsides in extravagant curves – curves that could never have been negotiated by standard gauge trains. Even then, a long train would normally have two Pacific class locomotives to provide the power. This provides spectacular scenery, hence the addition of the observation coach, though it had only limited seating for thirteen passengers in comfortable armchairs.

New steel coaches were introduced in 1937 in a blue livery at which point the Union Limited officially became the Blue Train. Services were interrupted by the Second World War but resumed in 1946 and by 1955 the steam locomotives were retired

The Union Limited train of South Africa in the mountains. To cope with the steep climbs and sharp bends, this was a narrow gauge route.

and replaced by electric locomotives. The service continues to run today, from Cape Town but now extended to Pretoria.

Not every long distance train offered comfortable accommodation and gourmet meals. Peter Fleming, writing about a second journey on the Trans-Siberian Express in his book, *One's Company* (1934) gives a very jaundiced account of his experience. He found the whole journey desperately boring but worst of all was the dining car:

> On each table there still ceremoniously stood two opulent black bottles of some unthinkable wine, false pledge of conviviality. They were never opened, and rarely dusted. They may contain ink, they may contain the elixir of life. I do not know. I doubt if anyone does.
>
> Lavish but faded paper frills still clustered coyly round the pots of paper flowers, from whose sad petals the dust of two continents perpetually threatened the specific gravity of the soup. The lengthy and trilingual menu had not been revised: 71 per cent of the dishes were still apocryphal, all the prices were exorbitant. The cruet, as before, was of interest rather to the geologist than to the gourmet. Coal dust from the Donetz Basin, tiny flakes of granite from the

> Urals, sand whipped all the way from the Gobi Deseret – what a fascinating story that salt-cellar could have told under the microscope! Nor was there anything different about the attendants. They still sat in huddled cabal at the far end of the car, conversing in low and disillusioned tones, while the chef du train, a potent gnome-like man, played on his abacus a slow, significant tattoo.

Unable to speak to the attendants in their language, he attempted to mime that he would like a boiled egg, only to be presented three-quarters of an hour later with a whole roast chicken.

Today, there are luxury trains running on every continent, but their nature has largely changed. In the earlier years, they were primarily intended to serve the same purpose as other passenger trains, take people from one place to another that they needed to reach. The new generation are not primarily about getting from A to B – they are, in a sense the destination. People join them to experience the journey. Some use old rolling stock to provide a nostalgic experience, but others have designed everything in their own, new styles and few are as stylish as the Seven Stars Cruise Train of Japan, designed for and built in the twenty-first century. There are just seven cars, but each has its own special character. One contains a Lounge Bar with panorama windows and a pianist to entertain the guests as they enjoy their drinks. In complete contrast is the Tea Room, which is very much the traditional Japanese, though it is in the *ryurei* style, which means that those who use it can sit in chairs, rather than having to kneel on the floor. There is another bar on board and a souvenir shop. A guest room can be used by ten pairs of guests. Accommodation is in suites, all air conditioned with their own showers and toilets, and two are deluxe suites, one of which at the very end of the train has a panoramic window. What, one wonders, would the Canadian writer who marvelled at the sleeping car of 1857 have made of this train? Trains such as the Seven Stars are not cheap – at the time of writing the cost of a two-day trip on the Seven Stars with one night on board is going to set you back at least $2,500. So, this is very much a trip for the wealthy. But it is not only the wealthy who have been able to enjoy better travel conditions as railway carriage construction moved on from the nineteenth century.

Chapter 7

CARRIAGE DEVELOPMENT IN THE TWENTIETH CENTURY

In Britain, side corridor trains dominated main line traffic throughout the first half of the twentieth century, but there was more standardisation following the grouping of 1923. Before that date there had been a proliferation of small companies that were now mainly amalgamated into just four: The Southern (SR), the Great Western (GWR), London North Eastern Railway (LNER) and the London Midland & Scottish (LMS). While the companies generally used steel underframes, there were differences in the coachwork. The LMS and LNER mainly stayed with the traditional wooden frames and wooden panels, the SR and GWR had converted to using metal panels in a wooden frame. The LMS, however, was unusual in introducing open third class carriages, which were notable for being ornate rather than plain, with tables between the seats. These latter were useful following another innovation, the introduction of buffet cars in the 1930s offering drinks and snack rather than the full meals of the dining cars.

The Pullman specials had been established earlier, but now the companies began providing sets of special coaches for their named trains. The LNER introduced their Silver Jubilee train in 1935, replaced by the Coronation Train to mark the accession of George VI in 1937. The train had a standardised arrangement of carriages in the following order behind the tender – brake third, kitchen third, two open firsts, open third kitchen, open third brake and observation car. The new coaches had interiors in the fashionable art deco style and were given a bright blue livery. The train was generally headed by one of Gresley's A4 Pacifics, also in a blue livery – the most famous locomotive that can be seen in this livery is, of course, the world record breaking *Mallard*. The train ran between London and Edinburgh, with a journey time of just 6 hours

The rather luxurious interior of an LMS third class carriage of the 1920s. It was unusual for British trains of the period to have open coaches.

northbound, but taking an extra half hour for the southbound journey. The rival on the west coast route to Glasgow was the LMS Coronation Scot. The light music composer Vivian Ellis was inspired, while travelling by train, to write an orchestral piece depicting the experience of travelling by express train, and he called it *Coronation Scot*. It was an immediate success and in 1938 it was adopted as the signature tune for the BBC radio detective series *Paul Temple*.

These special express trains were the ones that attracted the most attention, but they only represented a small part of the passenger traffic in Britain. Branch lines were often as busy as main lines. Even then, there were parts of the country

A promotional postcard showing a first class coach of the Coronation Express.

that were not served by any rail links, simply because the expense of building track and running costs was too great. One answer to that problem was the Light Railway Act of 1896. This allowed companies to build railways without the huge expense of receiving an Act of Parliament – they would get a Light Railways Order. The track could be lighter than usual and did not necessarily have to be built to the standard gauge. Restrictions were less stringent and facilities inferior to those offered in other parts of the system. Speeds on these lines were slower than on others. It was an inferior system in those respects, but the whole point was that it enabled communities to get rail connections that would otherwise be unavailable. Many of them were built as narrow-gauge lines. Statistics produced at the time showed that the cost of laying standard gauge on level ground varied between £2,392 and £3,987 per mile, while for 2ft 6in gauge it was £1,260 and £2,057. Narrow gauge, however, was not new – the first had been built in the tramway age, when horses, not locomotives, worked the line.

The Festiniog Railway (now the Ffestiniog) was opened in 1836 but the first steam locomotives only came into use in the 1860s and at this time the line was entirely used for freight, carrying slate from Blaenau Ffestiniog to the harbour at Portmadoc (Porthmadog) but soon afterwards started running passenger trains, as it still does today. The early years sound quite interesting as the track offered a decidedly uncomfortable ride at first. A contemporary account of travelling on the footplate of one of the earliest engines on the line, the *Little Giant* of 1867 makes alarming reading: 'Over the old portions of the road a speed of 8 or 9 miles an hour is the greatest at which it is possible to run without incurring the risk of breaking the springs or loosening the driver's teeth.' For the passengers in the swaying coaches, it must have been quite alarming as they passed through narrow cuttings, only a few inches away from rock walls. It has to be said that travelling the line today is a far more comfortable experience.

It is impossible to describe a typical light railway carriage, simply because there is no such thing. They had a bewildering variety of vehicles in use. Some were quite conventional, though usually rather spartan, often with unupholstered wooden seating. Others were quite open-sided and a few lines that had no bridges across the tracks were able to run double-decker carriages. All were conventional in any other

The Festiniog Railway probably in the 1870s, with two trains passing at Tan-y-Bwlch. One is a passenger train, the other a mixed passenger and goods.

respects, with the exception of the Listowel & Ballybunion Railway of Ireland opened in 1888. This was a monorail system, designed by a Frenchman, originally intended for use in the North African desert, but built in Ireland by a German engineer. The train had to be balanced. The locomotive had two cabs and two boilers, one each side of the rail. Similarly, carriages were divided one compartment to each side, and station staff had to direct passengers where to sit so that there were the same number on each side. This remarkable railway ran for some forty years, and has recently been recreated, but run by a new diesel locomotive.

The light railways were built to save money and to make it possible to run services in rural areas, where passenger numbers were comparatively small. But the same search for economy also applied to many branch lines, which led to the development of a new type of rail transport – the introduction of rail motors. Essentially these were composite vehicles, the locomotive section incorporated with the single

The narrow gauge Lynton & Barnstaple Light Railway winding its way round a hillside. Opened in 1898, it closed in 1935.

The extraordinary Listowel & Ballybunion monorail system at Listowel. The turntable in the foreground gave access to sidings.

carriage. On some lines, the small footplate and boiler unit was visible at the front, but the GWR cars kept the working part out of sight – only a stubby chimney poking through the roof gave it away. The GWR ran a route through the Golden Valley, the area between Stroud and Swindon, with numerous halts along the way. There was no need for station staff, as the guard sold tickets on board. They had the advantage that they could be worked in both directions on the line, without the need for the locomotive to run round the train. In one direction, the driver and fireman were in their usual positions on the footplate, but for the return journey, the fireman stayed where he was, but the driver moved to a compartment at the opposite end of the train, where there were controls mechanically linked back to the engine. The seats were like those already in use in street trams with backs that swivelled, so that the passengers were always looking forward, no matter which direction the train was travelling. They were popular with village communities, who no longer had to make their way to the nearest town to catch a train, but they suffered from the disadvantage that they were generally underpowered – rarely able to haul a second coach. However, they found use in many different countries for a time. In the early twentieth century, other alternative sources of power became available.

Restored GWR
Steam rail car on the West Somerset Railway.

As early as 1831, Michael Faraday had demonstrated the connection between magnetism and electricity. If you move a wire in a magnetic field, an electric current will be produced – the basis of the generator. Conversely, if you pass electricity through a wire, you can move a magnet – the electric motor. When asked by Gladstone what use this electricity might be, Faraday famously gave an answer to gladden any politician's heart. 'One day, sir, you may tax it.' It was to be over half a century, however, before the first electrically powered locomotive took to the tracks. In 1879, Werner Von Siemens demonstrated an electric locomotive at the Berlin Trade Exhibition. It was a miniature railway, in which the driver sat on the tiny engine, but it did show the possibilities of electric traction. One man who was impressed was Magnus Volk, who in 1883 got permission to run an electric railway along the seafront at Brighton. It was built to a 2ft 8½in gauge and power was supplied by a Siemens generator, worked by a gas engine. Electricity was supplied at 40 amps and 60 volts to the two rails, and powered a 60 horse power engine that produced a modest speed of 10 m.p.h. As originally run, there were open carriages and a special non-smoking saloon that was very exotic, with a painted ceiling, upholstered seats, silk curtains and gilt-edge mirrors. The train proved very popular and still runs today, but not, alas, with the luxury saloon.

Encouraged by the initial success, Volk decided he would like to extend his railway to Rottingdean, but inconveniently there were high cliffs in the way, so he decided to lay tracks on the shore. But there was a problem; they would be underwater at high tide. His solution was to build a carriage on stilts and to provide the power through overhead cables. The carriage was if anything even more elaborate than the earlier saloon, looking rather like a Victorian conservatory with stained glass windows. It was not a great success and disappeared after only a decade in use.

Volk's electric railway running along the seafront at Brighton.

The imposing façade of Lime Street station Liverpool by S. Kelper, engraved in 1831. The façade has been preserved, but the station behind it has been totally changed.

Above: The first class refreshment room at Swindon in the nineteenth century: alas nothing this splendid now exists.

Right: The entrance to the São Bento station, Porto, Portugal is famous for its polychrome tiles depicting local scenes and historical events.

Above: Originally known as the Victoria Terminus, Mumbai's main railway station is an exotic mixture of styles, often referred to as Hindu-Gothic.

Left: A nineteenth century advert for Pullman dining cars: the gentlemen passengers seem to be well supplied with liquid refreshment.

Above: The extravagant carriage built for Maximilian II and later used by King Ludwig in the Nuremberg Transport Museum.

Right: A cartoon from 1901 in which the attendant is saying: 'Say, Boss, if the public won't pay us our wages, I guess the Company'll have to do it.'

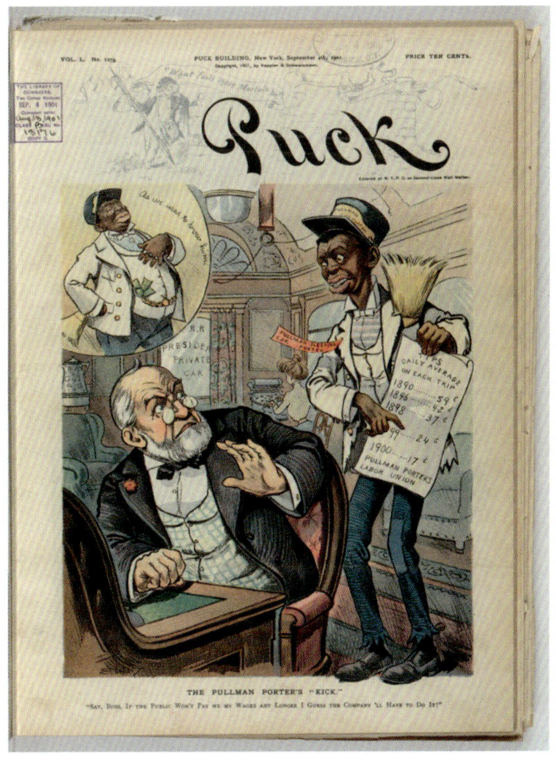

The rear compartment of the twenty-first century Seven Stars Train of Japan provides its occupants with this immense window.

The 'Flying Hamburger' diesel railcar at Leipzig station.

Above left: Escalators were such a novelty in early twentieth century London that they appeared in glamorous posters such as this.

Above right: The New Jersey resort was developed by the Camden Atlantic line, part of the Pennsylvania Railroad complex.

The ornate Komolskaya station on the Moscow Metro.

The original locomotive used on the Mount Washington cog railway now preserved on site.

The magnificent view of the Alps from the summit station of the Brienz-Rothorn Railway.

The New Jersey resort was developed by the Camden Atlantic line, part of the Pennsylvania Railroad complex.

The modern Glacier Express with its special glass domed carriages that ensure passengers get the possible view of the dramatic scenery.

A train on the Durango & Silverton Railroad passing above the Animas Canyon in Colorado.

The Harz Railway in Germany; the train is approaching the summit of the mountain line.

An international railroad experience. Two Chinese QJ Class locomotives head an American excursion train seen here crossing the Iowa River.

Italy's magnificent Arlecchino train of 1960 now offers special excursions on some of the country's most beautiful lines.

Volk extended his electric system to Rottingdean by means of this electric train on stilts, with current fed through overhead cables. It was not a success.

Volk's experiments did not lead to any immediate enthusiasm for developing the idea of electric railways, but by the beginning of the twentieth century things began to change. For a time, there was a dispute over the best way to provide the current to the motor, via a middle rail or by overhead wires. The latter has proved to be the more successful for conventional railways. Many countries began to adopt the new system. In America there was a modest start with electrification through a tunnel at Baltimore in 1895 but large scale operations only got under way in 1905 when the Long Island Railroad began a service from Brooklyn and Manhattan. Many early electric railways were used on suburban routes – in Britain, for example, these were mostly in the Southern region. But by the 1930s things had changed. America got its first main line electric system, when work began on the whole route between New York and Washington, using overhead conductors and alternating current. The 1930s saw widespread electrification in Europe, bringing economy, high speeds and comfortable rides.

Pacific Electric Railway—Five-Car Train as Regularly Operated

The Pacific Electric Railway Company of California was founded in 1901 and ran trains based on Los Angeles and San Bernadino.

Another possible power source had been developed in the nineteenth century. Rudolf Diesel took out a patent for a new type of internal combustion engine, in which the heat generated by compressing air in a cylinder was used to ignite oil pumped into the combustion chamber. The diesel engine proved a success with heavy road vehicles, but it was not immediately obvious how it might be used on the railways. Transmission presented a problem with long, heavy trains, but the engine could be used on rail cars, where they would immediately be more effective than the low-powered steam units already in use. They became common in many countries, but mostly for use on short runs. Among the early successful stories was the development of a high speed rail car in Germany in the 1930s which ran between Berlin and Hamburg, a route that gave it the name the 'Flying Hamburger', which sounds quite comic now, but there was nothing comical about its performance. It was capable of speeds over 100mph and covered the 178 mile journey from Berlin at an average speed of 77mph. The shape of the train was entirely new, with a very sleek appearance and a rounded front, the result of extensive tests in the wind tunnel normally used for testing Zeppelins. Where the earlier steam-powered railcars had been spartan, the Flying Hamburger was able to offer a far greater degree of comfort and extra facilities. There was just the one passenger compartment but divided into two halves. On one side of the corridor were pairs of seats facing one another, each able to seat three passengers, while on the opposite side of the aisle were single seats. In between the two sections was a small bar, and once the train was under way, a waiter appeared offering drinks and refreshments and providing small folding tables. The trains continued, with modifications, in use until the 1950s. One set is preserved at Leipzig station.

Streamlining became a feature of American railroads in the 1930s. There was a problem with American trains that so often had to cover long distances, far greater than those of any European country. Journey times that had once seemed wonderful, were less impressive in the age of the motor car and the bus. Although trains might have top speeds of up to 80mph, on the long routes there were stops to take on water and coal, and sometimes to change locomotives, all of which slowed progress down. And they looked much as they had twenty years earlier, with few improvements in carriage design and often decked out in rather dull liveries. Two companies set out to produce streamlined trains, powered by internal combustion engines. The first to be ready was the Union Pacific whose coaches were built by Pullman, but in a very different style from the familiar Pullmans already in use. These had riveted aluminium bodies and were given a bright yellow and brown livery. The new carriages were around a third of the weight of conventional coaches of similar size. Inside, the changes were equally striking and included air conditioning throughout and specially coated glass on the windows to reduce glare. Originally it was to have been hauled by a Winton diesel engine, but when the coaches were ready, the engines were not yet available. The Union Pacific was determined to be first in the field with the new style trains, so they hired a locomotive for a publicity tour. The newly named *Streamliner* started its journey on 12 February 1934. For those who saw it, the train was a revelation and seemed to epitomise modernity. It was designed with a top speed of 90mph and carried enough fuel to travel hundreds of miles non-stop.

The other company was the Chicago, Burlington & Quincy, and when their train *Zephyr* did finally appear, two months after the *Streamliner,* and made its promotional tour, it was even more of a sensational success. It was the epitome of modernity, with its sleek lines and unpainted steel locomotive and carriages. Like the *Streamliner,* it offered passengers a uniquely comfortable ride with a wide range of amenities. It also offered a brand new power system. The diesel engine did not drive the locomotive directly but worked a generator to provide electricity – the world's first diesel-electric locomotive. The success of the two trains brought a rush of other companies building streamlined trains of their own. Not all of them opted for diesel or diesel-electric. The Milwaukee Road's Hiawatha was steam hauled by an Atlantic 4-4-2 locomotive that enabled it to run a rake up to nine coaches long. Among its original features was the 'Skytop Lounge' at the rear of the train and a cocktail bar that was only possible thanks to the end of Prohibition.

One of the other famous streamliners, the Twentieth Century Limited, actually began its working life in a more conventional fashion in 1902, but even then was moving away from the elaborate decoration of the previous century, as a publicity announcement made clear. There was 'an absence of all heavy carvings, ornate grilles and metal work, stuffy hangings etc.' The new streamlined version appeared

The Burlington & Quincey Railroad *Zephyr* first ran in 1934 and with its streamlined metal body epitomised modernity.

A radio car on a Canadian National Railways train in the 1930s, in which passengers could listen to broadcasts through headphones.

in the 1930s and the train made its last run on its regular route between New York and Chicago in December 1967. On board for the last run were Rogers E.M. Whitaker and Anthony Hiss and they described the experience in their book *All Aboard with E.M. Frimbo* (1974). Although the famous train and the suite they shared showed signs of wear and tear, their description shows just how comfortable travel was even then, when the train was well past its best:

> It had metal walls painted grey, a large brown armchair with an antimacassar, a smaller brown armchair without an antimacassar, a red rug with a faded floral design, a small separate bathroom, an even smaller closet, and a picture window, which needed washing. On the seat of the large armchair was a brochure informing us that we would receive complimentary champagne with our dinner and complimentary newspapers and boutonnieres with our breakfast, that we could have our shoes shined and our suits pressed, and that, if we wanted them, a typewriter and an electric shaver were available.

Movement between countries and districts separated by wide expanses of water called for special measures. Train ferries date back to the beginning of the railway age, when the Monkland and Kirkintilloch Railway used a boat to take wagons from the line across the Forth & Clyde Canal. Ferries were also used to cross the Firth of Forth before the completion of the famous bridge. Europe was to see far more important and longer crossings, especially in the Baltic. Passengers in Britain heading for Copenhagen could take the ferry from Harwich to Esbjerg on the Jutland coast where they could board a through sleeper train for the rest of the journey. The first fifty-five miles take the train to the Little Belt, where the coaches are loaded onto the ferry for the two mile crossing. In the 1930s it took roughly twenty minutes to load the coaches, twenty minutes for the crossing and a quarter of an hour to get everything reassembled for the next part of the land journey to the sixteen mile wide Great Belt, where the crossing took around an hour and three quarters to reach Korsoer and the final run into Copenhagen. It was said that passengers using the sleeper service were not even aware they had even been on board a ship at all. Later a further train ferry service was inaugurated linking Copenhagen to Malmö in Sweden. The crossing of the Little Belt became redundant with the building of a bridge in the 1930s.

The most impressive ferry services of the early twentieth century linked Germany to Denmark and to Sweden. The latter was the longer of the two and was inaugurated in 1907 with four ships, two Swedish and two German. They were all of a similar size, fitted with two tracks, each able to take four coaches. Loading and unloading was simplified by ballast tanks on the ships that could be used to bring the tracks on board level with the tracks on land. Keeping the carriages secured required a complex system of shackles and screws. Passengers on board for the 58-mile crossing had a choice. They could stay in their carriages and electric bells were fitted so that they could call for stewards if they needed them. Alternatively, they could make use of the ship's own facilities that included cabins that held 140 passengers and the usual range of dining saloons and lounges. There is still a train ferry service between Germany and Sweden, but the modern service runs via Denmark. One other early train ferry deserves a special mention, the crossing of the Carquinez Strait in California. The ferry *Salarno* stated operating in 1878 and continued in use right through to 1930 when the Southern Pacific built a bridge. It not only took the passenger coaches but the engine as well.

The outbreak of war in Europe in 1939 that soon spread to become a world-wide conflict brought development to a halt in civilian rail transport. The post war years were difficult for many countries. Britain had huge debts to pay off and had little cash for investment. There was, however, a major structural change – the railways were nationalised in 1948. There was no longer competition between different companies, but modernisation did not get under way until the 1950s. In the rest of Europe there was war damage to be

The train ferry across the Carquinez Strait in California in the 1920s was unusual in taking locomotives as well as carriages. It closed in 1930 when a bridge was built.

repaired, but in America things were very different. There new ideas could be tried out.

One type of carriage that has not been discussed so far is the double-decker. In general, they cannot be used in Britain as a result of the large number of low bridges and tunnels, but they were used briefly on the line from Swansea to the Mumbles. Apart from that, the earliest examples came from France towards the end of the nineteenth century. The first were the *voitures à impériale* that were conventional carriages but with seats on the roof with open sides and just a canopy for shelter. They were succeeded by genuine double-deckers introduced on the Chemins de fer de l'Est. In these, the floor of the bottom compartment was lower than was usual on a carriage and the upper section was completely enclosed.

An early example of a double decker rail carriage, a voiture à impériale built for the Chemin de fer de l'Est and on show on the Champs Elysée.

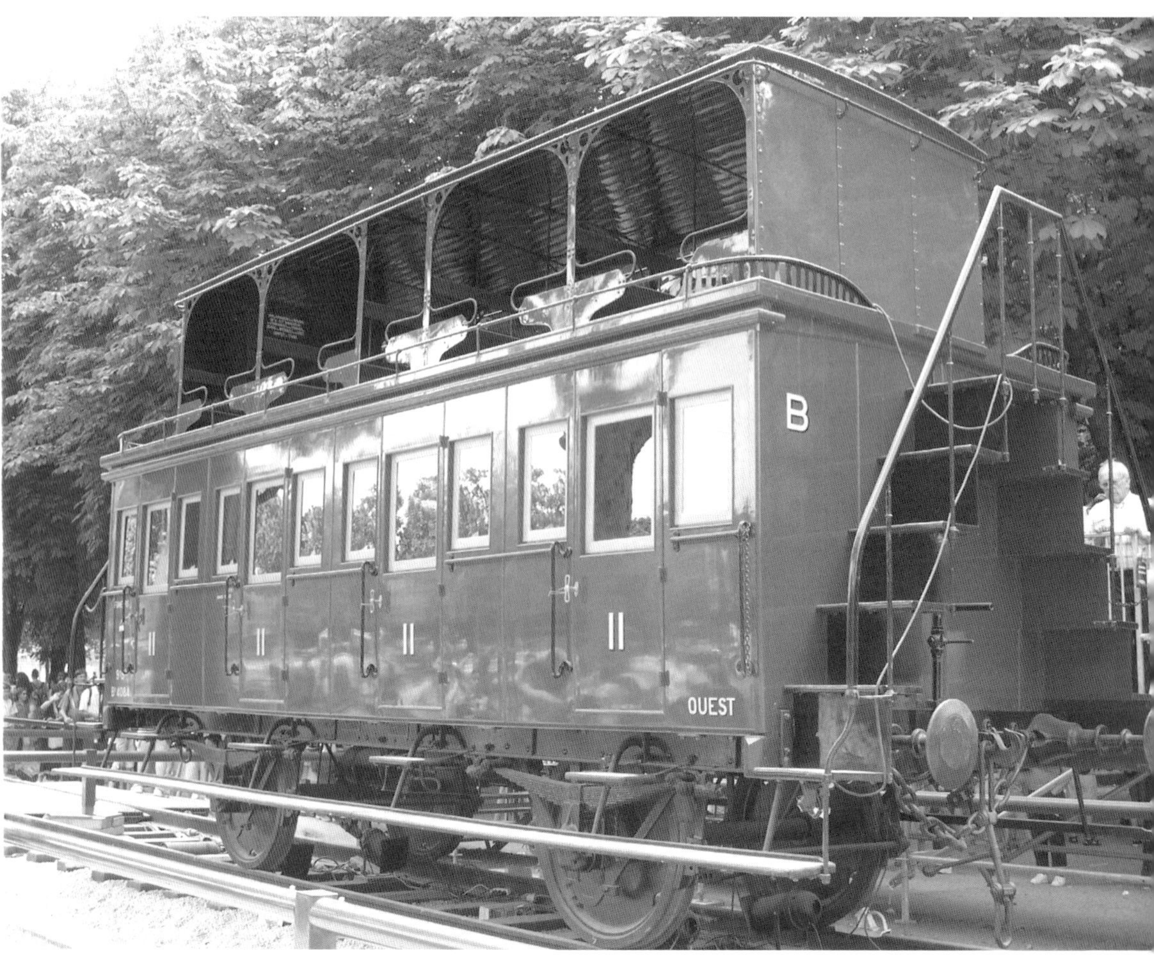

The real heyday of the double decker, however, was to come in the twentieth century. In 1950, the Chicago, Burlington & Quincey Railroad introduced the new stock on a suburban route in Chicago, but shortly afterwards the Atchison, Topeka & Santa Fe went one step further with new carriages for their El Capitan streamliner service. A number of European countries also adopted double-deckers

The advantages for the operating companies come in the shape of economy – much of the weight of the carriage is in the underframe – if one can get twice as many passengers on the same frame without doubling the weight that is an obvious advantage. There is a real bonus for the traveller as well. A few years ago, when I was researching locations for the Discovery TV Series *On the Rails,* I flew to San Francisco and my next stop was to be at the excellent railway museum

A German electric double decker train on the Hohenzollern Bridge, Cologne.

in Sacramento. The company were going to book the usual hire car for me, but I opted to take the train instead, and it was a surprise and delight when the double-decker rolled in. The top deck really does give you a much better view of the landscape than you get from lower down – and the fact that the bar was up there as well was an added bonus.

The main change in the second half of the twentieth century was the elimination of the steam locomotive from main line service. British Rail built its last, appropriately named *Evening Star* in 1960, though steam lingered on longer in some parts of the world – visiting India in the 1980s it was a surprise to find that every train passing through Delhi station was steam hauled, though plans for electrification were already under way. In Britain, meanwhile, the first big change came with the introduction of diesel multiple units (DMU) for shorter journeys. The interiors were on the open plan, with seats very similar to those used in buses of the period with tubular frames and less than luxurious upholstery. One novelty for passengers when they first appeared in the 1950s was that those sitting at the front could look past the driver to see the track unfold in front of them. The DMUs were a success and many are still in use today.

A far greater change came with the introduction of diesel power for express trains, culminating in the arrival of the Inter City 125 in the 1970s, named after its top speed of 125mph. It looked and was quite different from anything else that had been seen on British tracks. There was a diesel power unit at each end, and in between a rake of newly designed coaches. These were all open air-conditioned carriages with a variety of seating, some with tables between facing seats, others with drop-down tables attached to the seats in front. By this time, many railway companies had recognised that there was no longer a great demand for formal meals in a special dining car and as a result the 125s were designed with self-service buffet cars. Half a century later many of these units are still in use, a remarkable record.

One of the problems faced by British engineers attempting to design high speed trains was the track itself, first laid out in the Victorian age with what at the time seemed perfectly manageable bends. An attempt was made to overcome the problem with the Advanced Passenger Train, that tilted as it went round corners. It was not a success – passengers complained of feeling sick and there were technical problems – but it did succeed in achieving a new British speed record of 162mph. Britain was not alone in developing tilting trains: Italian engineers began working on the Pendolino that was ultimately to go into service in many European countries. A different scheme was followed in France, where the Train à Grande Vitesse (TGV) was electric as were the famous Shinkansen or bullet trains of Japan. What distinguishes the latter, however, from all other schemes was the track. The Japanese rail system runs through mountainous country and in the early years this called for narrow gauge routes. When the idea of high speed trains was being discussed, it was recognised that this was a limiting factor, so a whole new system was constructed to the standard gauge of 4ft 8½in.

The Japanese maglev train on the route linking Shanghai to the international airport at Pudong.

The main change over the past half century as far as passengers are concerned is the increases in speed. Travelling in a 125 in Britain is otherwise not so very different an experience from that of taking a trip in TGV in France. One other new form of train was developed at the start of the twenty-first century, the maglev based on magnetic levitation. The track is laid with two rows of magnets of alternating polarities – south pole opposite north pole and so on. The train contains superconductive magnets that create a repulsive force that lifts the whole train to hover, clear of the track. The forward drive is supplied by a linear motor. The longest maglev system now in use is only 19 miles, connecting Shanghai to the international airport at Pudong, a journey that takes just 8 minutes. Speed is the essential attraction of the system and 400km/hr runs have been recorded. To date, there has been no great rush to install these systems on a large scale, mainly due to the huge expense of providing the track, but the Indian authorities are discussing building a major route to link Mumbai to Pune almost 100 miles away. If maglev does come into general use, then passengers certainly will notice the difference: trains can be built with broader carriages, rides will be smoother than on any other train and speeds will certainly be far greater than even the fastest currently available. That, however, is looking into an uncertain future. In the next chapters we shall be turning back the clock to look at some other historical developments in rail travel.

Chapter 8

COMMUTERS

The nineteenth century saw a steady growth in city populations and with it an ever- increasing volume of traffic blocking the streets. There was a partial answer provided by the development of omnibuses, but each omnibus only held a small number of passengers. And as the rail system grew, the problem only got worse. Many people now lived further away from the places where they worked as suburbs spread and developed. Railways could carry far more passengers than any other available transport system, but how could you build lines through crowded, urban housing? One solution was found at the very beginning of the age, when London got its first steam railway from central London to Greenwich. The London & Greenwich Railway received it Act in 1833 and was to be the first steam railway in the capital. Having decided that running the line through the area was impossible, the engineers took the decision to go over the top of the existing roads and houses on a viaduct that would stretch the whole length of the line, with an astonishing 878 arches, that were built using an estimated 80 million bricks. Like all other early railways, passengers were offered stage-coach type carriages for first class, semi-covered for second and open for third, while wealthy individuals could use their own carriages mounted on flat trucks. It was the first elevated railway, and decades were to pass before other elevated railways were to be built, and the first of them appeared on the other side of the Atlantic.

New York in the 1860s was one of the most densely developed cities in the world, with Manhattan almost entirely covered with buildings. The streets were crowded. In the 1820s a report in *Harper's Magazine* declared that a lady might have to wait up to half an hour for a break in the traffic so that she could cross the street, and 'even then she makes the crossing at any point below the Park at her peril'. There was

The original London Bridge station on the London & Greenwich Railway, with tracks heading away over the houses of London on an immense viaduct.

certainly little space left for a conventional railway, so the West Side and Yonkers Patent Railway company was formed, and operations began in 1868. On 3 July, the first train ran over the elevated line from the Battery on the southern tip of Manhattan to Cortlandt Street in the financial district. The *New York Times* reported:

> The car ran evenly from the Battery to Cortlandt-street, starting at a rate of five miles an hour, and increasing to a speed of ten miles. The Company does not pretend with its present machinery, to run the cars faster than fifteen miles an hour, but during the next few months will make arrangements for much more rapid motion.'

This first line was something of a curiosity. Designed by Charles T. Harvey, an engineer who had previously worked on canal construction, it consisted of just one track carried on a single line of columns. It was cable-hauled, using a continually moving looped cable, worked by a stationary engine – the system used for the famous San Francisco cable cars. Cars were attached by means of a claw that grabbed onto collars on the cable. There were problems from the start – cars couldn't always grasp the cable and it was found that having the return cable at ground level was not working. The latter difficulty was partly solved by changing it to track level. Running costs were high and by November 1870, the company collapsed and the assets were sold off for the very low price of $960 – $22,000 today. The new company became the Westside Patented Elevated Railway Company, and they were granted permission to use steam locomotives, but this required strengthening of the superstructure with extra supports. The new company suffered losses and once again the whole system was auctioned off and yet another new company was formed in 1871, The New York Elevated Railway Company. A second elevated railway company was formed that was to run on compressed air along 5th Avenue to 59th Street. The two lines were eventually amalgamated as the Manhattan Elevated Railroad.

The new line certainly made a big difference for people needing to move around the city, but it was a good deal less popular with those who were moving around at ground level. As one visitor to New York remarked, it 'gives the impression of constantly walking under a bridge'. It was even worse for those living in apartments near the tracks. Residents of a block on 6th Avenue, between 56th and 57th Streets, complained to the city authorities, 'trains run by their windows from 5 o'clock in the morning until 12 at night. The smoke and the steam drawn down ends up against their windows, so that for most of the time they are compelled to keep them closed.' Eventually, by 1903, the New York system, that had been greatly expanded, abandoned steam power in favour of electric. That removed one part of the problem, but there was nothing that could be done to remove the mass of superstructure over the streets.

By the middle of the twentieth century, the whole system began to be demolished. One of the last to be closed down,

The New York elevated railway at the Bowery from the Robert N. Dennis collection of stereo images, published in 1902.

was also the last to be opened. There were ground level lines in New York. The New York Central was one of them and had turned 10th Avenue into a fatal thoroughfare, with over 500 deaths recorded as the result of people being hit by trains. The first attempt to solve the problem was the creation of what became known as the 'West Side Cowboys' – railway employees on horseback who waved red flags to warn of approaching trains. By the 1930s, however, the city authorities had had enough, and it was decreed that the line had to be replaced by an overhead route, the West Side Overhead Railway. When that too closed down, the superstructure remained standing and there were long debates over what was to be done with it. Eventually a very happy solution was found, and today it is a 1.45-mile-long green park.

The other major American city to build an elevated rail system was Chicago. With a name almost as long as the track, the Chicago and South Side Rapid Transport System began operation over a 3½ mile long track in 1892. It was initially worked by steam locomotives and the rolling stock was very similar to that in use on conventional trains at the time, with wooden coaches, featuring veranda sections at the ends. Chicago got its first look at electric traction at the World Fair held in the city in 1893. That convinced the company to make the change and steam went out, replaced by an electric third rail system. From that point on, the system expanded rapidly and became generally known simply as 'The L'. Unlike the New York system it still exists today, covering over 200 miles and averaging more than 600,000 passengers on weekdays.

Berlin still has one of the largest elevated railway systems in Europe, construction of which started in 1896 and like other nineteenth century lines of this type was originally worked with steam locomotives. It is now part of a complex,

The 5th Avenue terminus of the Chicago elevated railway, c.1900, from the *Electric Railway Journal*.

integrated system, connecting surface rail and underground sections. The overhead routes are extensive and represent a very good way of seeing the city from a new perspective. The most spectacular feature on the Berlin urban network is the Oberbaumbrucke, a double decker bridge across the Spree, with cars and pedestrians at one level and trains at the other. It was built in 1896 in an elaborate Gothic style, a reminder that this site was once that of one of the main entrance gates into the city. During the Cold War years, it was also a boundary between East and West Berlin.

The Liverpool Overhead Railway was opened in 1893 and was the first of its kind to use light electric vehicles from the start. By the 1950s, however, the fundamental structure was in such a badly dilapidated state that the company could not afford to repair it. The line closed in 1956. Britain was, however, to get one more overhead railway. The London Docks had become largely redundant by the latter part of the twentieth century, as they were no longer able to accommodate the much bigger container ships and tankers that constituted most of the world's trade. It was decided

The Berlin overhead railway system in the early twentieth century. The lower route is the Annhalter Bahn, now part of the S-Bahn system; the upper is the Hochbahn, now part of the U-Bahn.

that the area should be developed as a new financial centre based on the Isle of Dogs. It needed a good transport system, and it was decided to extend the old London & Blackwall Railway by new viaducts, including one that went right over the old West India Dock. The new line was named the Docklands Light Railway and opened in 1987. With the huge development of the Canary Wharf area, creating a mini-Manhattan of high-rise office blocks, further extensions were needed. By 2011, the line had reached Stratford, close to the new Olympic Stadium. What set this line apart was the method of operation – the trains were computer controlled. It is a very odd experience to sit in the front of a train, where the driver's cab would normally be and not see any driver. The only member of staff on board is the Passenger Service Agent, who is responsible for opening and closing the doors, giving out information – and in an emergency taking over control.

The alternative to going above cities was to go under them. An underground railway for London had been proposed

The Dockland Light Railway. As can be seen in this photo, there is no driver in the cab.

as long ago as 1830, but nothing happened until the 1850s. More and more people were working in the city but living outside it and arriving by rail at the great main line stations in North London. They then needed to make their way to their offices in the City through the increasingly congested streets. Various schemes were suggested for solving the problem, but the one that was eventually agreed on was for the Metropolitan Railway that achieved an Act of Parliament in 1854. It would link Paddington to Farringdon in the City, with intermediate stations at Euston and King's Cross. Construction of the line was by 'cut and fill', in which a deep cutting was first excavated and then later covered over to create the underground line. The Great Western requested that track should be laid to the broad gauge so that their trains could use the system, and then the Great Northern asked for a third rail for their standard gauge trains. The line was given a short trial run on 24 May 1862. No coaches were yet available and the dignitaries, including William Gladstone, had to travel in contractors' trucks fitted with bench seats. It opened to the public in January 1863 and attracted huge crowds. They

London's Metropolitan Railway was originally used by both the Great Western and Great Northern Railways. Here we can see a GWR brad gauge train, with the third rail between the outer pair to allow standard gauge running.

travelled in eight-wheeled coaches hauled by a GWR steam locomotive.

There were problems in sharing the route between two companies and soon the Great Northern were producing their own locomotives and rolling stock. There is an obvious problem in having steam engines belching out steam, smoke and fumes in an underground railway. The GNR engineer John Fowler designed a new type of locomotive in which the steam, instead of being simply exhausted up the chimney, was led through a pipe to a tank where it was condensed back into water. That was a success. His other innovation was less so. There was a second firebox, a combustion chamber, filled with fire bricks. These were steam heated before the engine left. While working in the open, the locomotive worked conventionally, but on entering the underground section, the firebox damper was closed and the heat from the bricks used to raise steam. One result was that when running underground, the engine was very silent, just the clatter of wheels on rails, and earned it the name of 'Fowler's Ghost'. For passengers using the underground railway, it was not very different from using any other railway when running through a long tunnel. It was a great success, carrying over ten million passengers in the first year.

More underground railways soon followed. One of the first was quite different. It was the idea of Peter Barlow. Instead of using 'cut and 'fill', the new system would be in an underground tunnel, constructed using a tunnelling shield – a system already used successfully by Marc Brunel in constructing the first tunnel under the Thames. This line was also to run under the Thames, from Tower Hill to Southwark, and it would use cable haulage instead of locomotives to pull a single carriage back and forth. Steam powered lifts were used to reach the two ends of the tunnel. The charge was a modest penny a trip. It was a dismal failure, often breaking down and leaving terrified passengers stranded in the dark underneath the river. After just a few months, all the rails and machinery were removed and it became a pedestrian tunnel. That too closed down when Tower Bridge was built – no one wanted to walk through a dark, damp tunnel under the

Thames when they could walk over it in the fresh air. The old Brunel pedestrian tunnel itself was later to be adapted for use as part of the District Line.

Another line was promoted, with the intention of using cable haulage, The City of London & Southwark Subway Company, later to become just the City & South London. But as preparations were getting under way, successful experiments had been made with electric traction in 1889. This was successful and now the company had to build its own power house to provide the electricity, an immense affair with three 450 horse power steam engines used to power the generators that were equally massive weighing in at 17 tons each. Power was supplied to a third rail as a DC current at 500 volts and 450 amps. Each locomotive pulled a train of three wooden carriages that each seated thirty passengers on bench seats running down each side of the carriage. The carriage builders decided that as there was nothing to see in a tunnel, windows were unnecessary, part from ventilation slits at the tops of the carriages. Upholstery was run right up

The first generation of electric trains seen here at Stockwell station, with the locomotive at the left and the windowless carriages to the right of the island platform at Stockwell Station.

the sides of the carriages. Access was via sliding metal lattice doors. One of the carriages was a men only for smokers. There may have been nothing to see, but passengers found them claustrophobic and with the high upholstery backs, they got the popular name of 'padded cells'. There was no need for elaborate stations on the line – passengers paid a standard fare of twopence at a turnstile. The route was steadily extended an eventually became part of the Northern Line.

Other electric lines followed with somewhat better carriages. The District Line also had its own power station at Lots Road in Chelsea, the biggest then built for any railway at the time, with eight generators rated at 5500 kW. As the system spread, the padded cell types were abandoned, and all had windows, though bench seating was still the norm. One company, however, went one better. The London Electric Railway bought two Pullman type coaches, in which passengers could sit in comfortable armchairs and order refreshments – a luxury that was not to be seen again on the London Underground. As more tunnels were dug, longer and deeper, a new difficulty arose – how to get passengers to the trains, and more importantly, up again to the surface. A long set of stairs to go down might not be much of a problem – a long set to climb would be very different. Lifts have a limited capacity. The answer appeared in October 1911, when a new device was installed at Earl's Court Station – an escalator. This was based on a design by an American Charles Seeberger who developed it in association with the famous lift manufacturer, Otis. There was some initial concern about safety and use by people with walking difficulties, so the company hired a man with a wooden leg called Bumper Harris to go up and down as a test. The escalators had an admirable safety record until 18 November 1987, when a fire started on the escalator fitted with wooden treads at King's Cross. It was thought to have been caused by a lighted match dropping onto waste caught beneath the steps. Fire shot out into the booking hall, causing 31 deaths and over 100 were injured.

The effect of the spread of London and the development of the surrounding areas was immense. The Metropolitan Line would eventually reach out far from the centre, arriving right out as far as Amersham and Aylesbury, but still the company found that there were not quite enough commuters in the outer regions to provide profitable numbers of paying passengers. They decided they needed to build more houses and from 1919 onwards they built a grand total of 4,600 new houses in mock-Tudor style, creating what became known as Metro Land. House buyers did what the company had hoped they would do – they travelled on the Metropolitan Railway to go to work or to enjoy London night life.

As the system developed, it became more complex and maps were printed to help passengers get around. Rail maps were not new and they had always been designed much as other maps were, with distances between stations accurately represented, and the lines themselves shown just as they were below ground. The resulting Underground maps looked more like a maze than a guide. It was a graphic designer, Harry Beck, who realised in 1931 that, as there was nothing to see and distances between stations were short, there was no need to show actual routes and distances. All the passengers really needed to know was which line to take and where, if necessary, they had to change to a different line. He simplified everything down – all stations were spaced equidistantly and joined by straight lines – apart from obvious exceptions like the Circle Line. His map, though brought up to date when new lines were added, is the familiar map Londoners use to this day.

The success of the London system resulted in similar schemes being set up in major cities throughout the world. There was one notable difference between the Underground and other railways – there was no need for elaborate station buildings. Trains arrived at short intervals so waiting rooms were unnecessary. Space was always at a premium in cities, so at street level all that was really necessary was an access point, and booking halls could actually be quite small and set below street level. But the entrances needed to have easily recognised distinctive signs to identify them. London Underground eventually settled for the well-known circle with a bar across. The Paris Metro, by contrast, had elaborate ironwork signs in the Art Nouveau style. The interiors of the stations are generally rather plain – some might have decorative tiles or colourful posters. One set of undergrounds however went in for an almost Baroque splendour for their stations. Nowhere are there tube stations more elaborately decorated than in Russia.

The tube systems around the world have proved very successful but inevitably suffer from overcrowding at rush hour periods, when carriages are packed with sitting and standing passengers. Getting them all organised is generally left to the passengers themselves to get into the train as best they can, but in some places, staff help out. Tokyo, for example, is famous for its 'passenger pushers' cramming as many as possible into the carriages. This was needed simply because in the 1970s, the trains were running at over 200 per cent of their design capacity. Things have improved

Commuters on a crowded train heading into Mumbai.

in recent years. Not all commuters use either overground or tube networks but rely on conventional surface trains. That does not stop them suffering from the same problem of overcrowding. In India, for example, it is not unusual to find passengers outside as well as inside carriages.

The widespread use of the tube system has sometimes made it a target for a terrorist attack. In March 1995, members of a fanatical religious doomsday group, Aum Shinrikyo, launched attacks using sarin nerve gas on three lines in Tokyo, resulting in 13 being killed instantly and 1,000 suffering injuries, from which some died later. London, too, suffered an attack at the height of the morning rush hour on the District Line on 15 September 2017. A rather crude timed bomb in a bucket, hidden in a carrier bag, exploded and although many had to be treated for burns, there were no deaths. An Iraqi, Ahmed Hassan, was arrested and later found guilty. These are rare events. Travelling by tube is generally very safe – far safer than being out among the traffic on the roads and streets of the city.

Chapter 9

EXCURSIONS AND SCENERY

The first recorded excursions by train occurred on the pioneering Liverpool & Manchester Railway soon after its opening, with a trip to see the Sankey Viaduct in the Duke of Wellington's coach. Shortly afterwards, in May 1831, there was a special excursion organised for the Bennett Street Sunday school from Liverpool to Manchester at one third of the usual price. This set a pattern for early excursions, often organised by local churches. For example, in 1839, when the church authorities at Grosmont arranged a trip from there to the seaside town of Whitby. Not all were quite so wholesome. In 1836, the Bodmin & Wadebridge Railway ran an excursion to witness a public execution. The event is largely forgotten, but one excursion was to lead to the formation of a major travel organisation. Thomas Cook was walking from his home in Market Harborough to attend a temperance meeting in Leicester, fifteen miles away. He was half way there when, in his own words, 'A thought flashed through my brain, what a glorious thing it would be if the newly-developed powers of railways and locomotion could be made subservient to the promotion of temperance!' He suggested his plan to the meeting, which approved it, and afterwards he went to see John Fox Bell, the Secretary of the Midland Counties Railway Company, who agreed to lay on a special train on 5 July 1841:

> Mr. Paget, of Loughborough, opened his park for a gala, and on the day appointed about five hundred passengers filled some twenty or twenty-five open carriages – they were called 'tubs' in those days – and the party rode the enormous distance of eleven miles and back for a shilling, children half-price. We carried music with us, and music met us at Loughborough station. The people crowded the streets, filled windows, covered the house-tops, and cheered us all along the line, with the heartiest welcome.

> All went off in the best style and in perfect safety we returned to Leicester, and thus was struck the keynote of my excursions, and the social idea grew upon me.

Cook went on to organise more rail excursions, at first mainly for temperance meetings and Sunday school outings. But by 1845, he had organised his first purely commercial trip to Liverpool. The opening of the Great Exhibition at the Crystal Palace in London's Hyde Park in 1851 brought in a lucrative trade. Cook claimed that in all he had taken 165,000 passengers to London to see it. Thomas Cook & Son went on to become an internationally famous firm of travel agents. When a new headquarters building was completed in Leicester in 1894, significant events were carved into the frieze, starting with the humble temperance excursion and including a more exotic paddle steamer on the Nile.

The problem with early excursions was coping with large numbers when carriages were small and locomotives not particularly powerful. In 1844 a train set off from Leeds for

The carved frieze at the top of the Thomas Cook office building in Leicester, showing an excursion train and the Crystal Palace.

Hull with 6,600 excursionists in 240 carriages – an immense train that required the services of nine locomotives. Many of these trains were so overworked that they were unable to keep to their schedules, and passengers had scarcely time to enjoy their destination before it was time to hurry back to the station for the train home.

In the industrial towns of northern England, an old religious celebration had taken on a new significance. Wakes had been held as vigils, followed by sports and games, but in the early nineteenth century their character changed and they became purely secular events. Wakes weeks were times when mills and factories closed for maintenance and repairs, leaving the workforce with time on their hands. To ensure there was a regular supply of the mill products, each major town used a different week, so that Wakes weeks were spread right across the summer months. It was a good time for excursions and seaside resorts were popular venues. Resorts had been developed in the eighteenth century not so much for fun and recreation, but because of a general belief that sea water was beneficial to health. This did not necessarily involve anything as adventurous as actually going in among the waves. Patrons of the resorts could bathe in tubs of sea water – and some medical professionals actually recommended drinking sea water. For industrial workers, however, the main attraction was the clean sea air and the contrast with the smoke and grime of their home towns. For Lancastrians, one town in particular proved a major attraction – Blackpool.

In 1801, the Blackpool census showed it as a mere hamlet with a population of just 473 but that began to change in the first half of the century and the big boost was the arrival of the railway in 1846. After that, the town boomed and attracted huge crowds who arrived on the excursion trains. By the latter part of the century, however, the weekly holiday became normal and the railway was kept busy throughout the summer months as the town added more and more attractions, with its piers and the famous Blackpool Tower. The industrial workers of Yorkshire also had their own favoured resorts. Redcar had, like Blackpool been a hamlet with a few fishing boats, but again the arrival of the railway in 1846 turned it into a thriving resort. Both towns catered for a basically working class population, with nearby resorts, Southport in Lancashire and Saltburn in Yorkshire, being favoured by the middle classes. Many large industries ran their own excursions. The Bass brewery at Burton-on-Trent, for example, began running day trips for its entire work force in the 1860s, later allowing them to bring their families along as well at very reduced cost. Each worker got their full day's wages plus a little extra pocket money. Typical destinations were Scarborough and Blackpool, with as many as 10,000 being taken in up to seventeen special rains, leaving at fifteen minute intervals.

The older resorts that had been popular in the eighteenth century, such as Brighton, also thrived in the railway age and were regularly served by excursion trains. Railway companies recognised that this was a very popular movement and as more and more people began to enjoy paid holidays, they actively promoted resorts and the trains that served them. Cornwall became a popular destination and the GWR reached Penzance from London in 1867, though it was a long journey time of at least 9 hours. Faced by competition from the London & South Western Railway, they introduced a new express train that took just 5 hours for the journey, with connections to Falmouth and St Ives. It was given a new and glamorous name – it was the Cornish Riviera Express. Britain was, of course, not the only country to develop seaside resorts.

In America it was not just the grime of industry from which people hoped to escape, but the summer heat of the cities. Abescon Island off the coast of New Jersey only got its first European permanent resident in 1783, but others followed and in 1850, Dr Joseph Pitney decided that its beaches and equable climate made it just the place for a popular resort – provided people could reach it easily. The answer was the Camden-Atlantic Railroad, from Camden, just outside Philadelphia, that would offer easy access from both that city and New York. The line was authorised in 1852 and as work began on laying tracks, so architects and engineers set about developing the resort, which was ready to receive visitors when the first train arrived in 1854. By this time, it also had a name; it was to be called Atlantic City. It became hugely popular and in its heydays in the 1920s was a regular

Nineteenth century sheet music cover suggesting that while cheap excursions to the seaside might have been fun they were not necessarily comfortable.

stopping point for shows enjoying trial runs before opening on Broadway.

Escaping uncomfortable weather did not always mean heading for the seaside. In India, the British found the heat of the plain in summer to be quite overwhelming. They headed inland rather than to the coast, to the cool of the hills. Popular hill stations such as Simla (now Shimla) and Darjeeling were originally reached by tortuous roads winding up the hills. Railway building was always going to be a problem, and both destinations were only reached by narrow gauge tracks. The Darjeeling Himalaya Railway, opened in 1881, required a complex system of zig zags and loops to make its way up the foothills of the Himalayas. It has remained a popular tourist route, still using steam locomotives, though diesel engines are also in use.

One of the loops on the Himalaya Darjeeling Railway that allows trains to climb the steep hillside.

One reason that people still enjoy the train rides up to Darjeeling is that they relish the mountain scenery. That was not always the case. At the beginning of the eighteenth century, mountain areas were not greatly admired. Daniel Defoe made a tour of Great Britain, describing what he saw in books published between 1724 and 1726. When he reached the Lake District, all he could see were 'frightful mountains' and he was delighted to reach the 'flat country' which was 'pleasant, rich, fruitful'. All that had changed by the end of the century with the picturesque movement, which praised craggy hills and romantic ruins. By the nineteenth century, the Romantic movement had taken hold and people wanted to go to the wilder places – and even go to the tops of those 'frightful mountains' to enjoy the view. Not everyone was willing, or possibly able, to reach mountain tops. In the Alps, it was possible to arrange to be carried up the less demanding peaks in a litter, but that was hardly a very satisfactory form of transport. It was an American businessman Sylvester Marsh who first thought that the answer might be a mountain railway.

Marsh was on holiday in New Hampshire, and he much admired the scenery around Mount Washington, at 6,188ft (1,917m) the highest peak in the north east of America. His idea of running a railway up the mountain was generally greeted with disdain and mockery. However, he found two engineers, a father and son, Herrick and Walter Aiken who took him seriously and came up with a plan that would get a train up the mountain without resorting to a complex system of zigzags and loops. They would build a cog railway. This was not a new idea. It had first been used right at the beginning of the railway age. Richard Trevithick's pioneering locomotives had worked but had broken the brittle cast iron rails. John Blenkinsop of the Middleton Colliery near Leeds wanted to use steam locomotives to take coal to the Aire & Calder Canal but was aware of the problem. What he needed was a way of building a light locomotive but one that would have enough power for the job. With the engineer Matthew Murray he opted for a rack and pinion system, in which a rotating cog on the engine engaged with a toothed track, providing extra traction.

When it began operations in 1812, it was the world's first commercially successful steam railway.

Construction of the Mount Washington railway was a long process as all the material had to be brought to the site on ox carts via rough, woodland tracks. The original locomotive was a curious affair with a vertical boiler, and two sets of cogs connecting to double rack rails set between the running rails. It was given the sassy name *Old Pepperass*. The carriages were rudimentary, but the line was a success from the day it opened in 1869. It still runs today and though the original engine has been replaced, two steam engines are still in use – *Ammonoosuc* (1875) and *Waumbek* (1908).

At the same time as Marsh was planning his mountain route, a Swiss engineer was independently coming up with a very similar scheme. Niklaus Riggenbach was one of the pioneers of Swiss railway development, having driven the country's first locomotive in 1847. He became an executive of the Swiss Central Railway and in 1863 he began developing his own version of a rack railway. The first trials took place on his birthday on 21 May 1870 over an 800m length of track. When that proved successful a line was constructed from Vitznau to Rigi, eventually ending at a height of 1752m at Rigi Kulm. Riggenbach predicted it would attract 50,000 visitors a year but in the year following its opening in 1871, 60,000 turned up to enjoy the novel experience. Like the Mount Washington railway, it too was originally worked by a vertical boilered locomotive. In spite of its success, there were problems, with a noticeably rough ride. The solution was developed by another Swiss engineer, Carl Roman Abt. His system was patented in 1882. He used two racks, side by side, but out of phase, so that the tooth on one was opposite a gap on the other, evening out the motion. Today steam is no longer used on the Vitznau Rigi Railway, which was electrified in the 1930s. But tourists can still enjoy steam in the mountains on the next line, the Brienz-Rothorn.

It is an obvious choice for a railway as the view from the summit of the Rothorn offers a huge panorama of Alpine peaks. It was built using the Abt system. The locomotives may seem familiar to British visitors, as the company also supplied engines of the same type to the Snowdon Mountain

Railway. When standing in the station on the level, they look as if they are about to tip on their noses, but the design makes sense once they start to climb. The rear wheels are larger than the front so on the incline the boiler remains horizontal. It is a long climb to the summit and such hard work for the engine that it has to make a stop half way to take on more water. Like all mountain railways, the engine is always below the carriages as a safety measure. On the return journey, descending under gravity, the cylinders act as air brakes.

The steepest of all the Alpine railways – and the steepest anywhere in the world – is the Mount Pilatus. Begun in 1898, it seemed impossibly steep with a gradient of 1 in 2, and to overcome it a new form of traction was required. As well as the conventional rack and pinion, there is a central rail, gripped by horizontal wheels on either side. Today it is entirely worked by electric locomotives and I was fortunate enough to be offered a ride in the driver's cab. Starting the descent was rather like staring down from a roller coaster about to make one of its downward rushes.

Not all railways offering splendid mountain views head straight up to a summit. Le Train Jaune – the yellow train – for example in the French Pyrenees winds through the hills, crossing ravines on some spectacular viaducts, including the unusual Pont Gisclard, a suspension viaduct. The first section opened in 1904 and the 1km line was gradually extended and now runs for 63 km from Villefranche-Vemet-les-Bains to Latour-de-Carol-Enveitg. The line was electrified from the start, and in order to provide the current to the third rail, the company had to build its own hydro-electric plant. Where at various points it crosses roads on the level, intimidating signs warn of 'danger de mort' – danger of death. Travelling the line offers spectacular scenery and in the summer months, tourists can enjoy a journey in open carriages as well as the more conventional closed variety. There are numerous stations along the way, but they are request stops only. The vast majority of passengers are travelling just to enjoy the experience and, as my wife and I did, when reaching the end of the line simply get the train back to the start and enjoy the ride all over again.

The Pilatus Railway, the steepest mountain railway in the world. This is an early photo taken when it was steam-hauled; the line has now been electrified.

Today, trains that are designed specifically to offer travellers magnificent scenery are big business. The Rocky Mountaineer, for example, offers a variety of journeys through the Canadian Rockies using special coaches with glass domed roofs. The silver class passengers get a single level carriage, but those paying for the gold leaf service get a double decker where the top deck is fully glazed offering uninterrupted views. A similarly scenic service has been offered since the 1930s on the Glacier Express, linking the two famous Swiss resorts of Zermatt and St. Moritz. The name 'Express' might seem something of a misnomer when the average speed is a sluggish 23mph, but the name simply signifies it is a non-stop route. Those who book to travel the line are certainly not going to worry about travelling at a speed that allows them time to take in the mountain scenery. At the start of the railway age, people took the train because they were in one town and needed to get to another. For those who travel the scenic routes, the journey itself is the attraction.

Chapter 10

ACCIDENTS

Accidents are, fortunately, comparatively rare on the railways, and can arise from many different sources, from human error to natural disasters. In the early days, some were caused simply by unfamiliarity with the new form of transport. The tragic death of Huskisson was described earlier, but it was a far less serious encounter that led to one important improvement in safety. In 1838, a train on the Leicester & Swannington Railway hit a horse and cart full of milk and eggs. No one was hurt though it must have created an almighty mess. The railway manager, Ashlin Bagster, suggested to George Stephenson that some sort of warning device on the locomotive might prevent such accidents, and the engineer proceeded to design the steam whistle, with a sound that would become synonymous with steam locomotives.

A problem in the early days was caused by the lack of power available, which some drivers tried to overcome by fastening down the safety valve, resulting in boiler explosions that might not have harmed the passengers but usually killed the footplate crew. That was prevented by making it impossible for anyone on the footplate to tamper with the device. Another of the issues faced by those responsible for running the railways was to ensure that trains did not run into each other. At first, it was thought to be enough simply to have a time gap between trains on the same line, which at the start of running on the Liverpool & Manchester was merely ten minutes. It was soon apparent that that alone was not enough, and railway employees were stationed at various points along the line to give hand signals to the drivers – one arm held horizontally indicated all clear, extended upwards, caution and both hands raised meant stop. At night they had to hang a white light from a pole as all clear and red for stop.

This proved to be wholly inadequate and mechanical signals were introduced, mainly of the semaphore type, where the position of the arm indicated what the driver was required to do. They were equivalent to the old hand signals, but for the all clear, the semaphore arm was left in a slot in the post. So, if a driver saw no signal, he was free to go ahead. The problem with this system was tragically illustrated on the Great Northern Railway on 21 January 1876. It was a foul day of driving snow when a slow goods train with thirty-seven coal trucks set off from Peterborough. Some way behind its stately progress, the Flying Scotsman was hurtling down the same track. The signalman was instructed to halt the goods train and shunt it into a siding to allow the express through. He duly set the signal but had no way of knowing that the arm had been frozen into its slot and the driver of the goods simply assumed he was free to continue. By the time the driver of the express had seen the train in front of him it was far too late to stop, and it ploughed into the back of it. That was not the end of the tragedy, for a second express then appeared and ran into the wreckage. Altogether fourteen were killed in the accident and twenty-four seriously injured.

Later the system was changed to avoid this ever happening again – the all clear was indicated by the arm being lowered below the horizontal. The biggest improvement came with the introduction of the electric telegraph that enabled signalmen in different boxes to communicate with each other. This was combined with the block system. When a train passed a box, the signal was changed to stop. No train could then be allowed to go forward again past that box, until the signalman received the telegraph message from the next box that the train had now cleared that section. Even so, accidents still did happen, sometimes due to confusion between the two signalmen. A classic case happened on the London, Brighton & South Coast Railway on 25 August 1861. Trains were being run at five minute intervals out of Brighton. First to leave was a sixteen coach excursion, followed by a seventeen coach excursion and finally a regular service train of twelve coaches. What follows is a complex story. To understand it there are two important points: there were signalmen at each end of the Clayton tunnel on the line, communicating by telegraph, but there was also an automatic system in use. When the train hit a treadle on the rail, it automatically turned the signal behind it to danger. If it failed to operate an alarm bell rang in the signal box. That was exactly what happened, but the signalman did not immediately respond to the bell, but did send the 'train in tunnel' message down the line. But by then, the next train had already passed the signal that had not been set to danger. The signalman leant out of his box, waving a red flag but saw the train disappear into the darkness. He had no idea whether the driver had seen him or not. It was now that everything got confused. When the signalman at the north end was asked if the train had cleared the tunnel, he reported it had. But he was referring only to the first train. In fact, the driver of the second had seen the red flag and had brought his engine to a halt half way down the tunnel. The south end signalman believing that both trains were now clear, allowed the third through with the inevitable result. In the carnage, 23 passengers were killed and 176 seriously injured.

The worst example of a collision between two trains in American history happened at Nashville Tennessee on 9 July 1918. One train, No.4, was leaving Nashville for Memphis, and the other, No. 1, was travelling in the opposite direction. Although most of the line was double track, there was a 10 mile section of single track, known as 'Dutchman's Curve'.

No.1 had the right of way over this section, so No.4 was required to wait until it had cleared before continuing on its journey. There were supposed to be two safety measures in place. The crew of the waiting train should not give the all clear until they had actually seen the other train leave the single track section and the signalman should only show the line clear sign when he knew everything really was in order. The conductor on No. 4 was busy checking tickets and he gave orders for others to look out for No.1. He was aware of another train leaving the single section and assumed that was actually the other passenger train but was in fact a quite different train of empty carriages. The signal board showed all clear, so No.4 headed off down the track. Too late, the signalman discovered the error and tried to stop the train by frantically blowing a whistle, but no one heard it. At 7.20 in the morning, the two trains met head on – one traveling at an estimated 50mph, the other at 60mph. The impact was tremendous and with wooden coaches not metal the destruction was terrible. The death toll was 101 and 171 were injured.

Today, there are far more efficient signalling system so that the chances of collisions have been hugely reduced. Yet on 28 February 2023, that is exactly what happened in Greece, between Thessaloniki and Larissa. A freight train was heading south. A train with 342 passengers on board from Athens was heading north and should have been on a quite different stretch of track, but for some reason was diverted onto the same line as the freight train, so that unknown to either driver they were heading straight towards each other at high speed. They met head on and the first two coaches of the passenger trains, full of students were totally demolished.

The accident at Nashville, Tennessee in 1918, when two trains collided head-on.

The wagons exploded into flames. In the chaos, passengers described being hurled through windows and struggling to escape from the smoke and flames. At the time of writing, 57 bodies had been recovered from the wreckage, but far more were expected to be found. Sixty-six had been taken to hospital. Quite how and why it happened will no doubt be revealed in a public enquiry, but it was reported that a stationmaster and three other men had been arrested.

Structural failures were a rare cause of accidents, but when they did occur, the effects were likely to be drastic. One of the earliest happened on the line being constructed to join Chester to Holyhead. The engineer Robert Stephenson had to design a viaduct to cross the River Dee. His first thought was a conventional five-arched brick viaduct but he eventually settled for a three-arch version, where the stone piers were joined by cast iron spans, supported by wrought iron ties. It was a method that had been successfully used for a bridge over the River Lea without causing any problems. But on 24 May 1847, the driver of a train crossing the bridge heard an ominous cracking sound. He at once opened up the regulator, and though the locomotive reached the far side before the bridge gave way, the connection to the tender broke and with it the rest of the train plunged into the river. The fireman who was on the tender at the time and a guard were killed, but miraculously only two passengers died, though sixteen were seriously injured. A public enquiry found that the bridge had been damaged due to a derailment by the train, but modern engineers point out that in fact the design was fundamentally flawed, largely because the wrought iron ties were actually so positioned as to be absolutely useless. Had the enquiry come to the same conclusion, then the career of one of Britain's greatest railway engineers could have been finished. In fairness to Stephenson it has to be pointed out that the railway engineers were having to solve problems never faced by earlier generations of bridge builders, who had to take structures carrying nothing much heavier than a horse and cart. Also, none of them had any formal training in engineering. Unlike France, Britain at the time had no engineering schools. But the Dee bridge disaster was as nothing compared to that of the Tay Bridge.

The engineer responsible for building the 2¾ mile bridge across the Tay at Dundee, the longest railway bridge of the time, was Thomas Bouch. He had originally planned a single lattice girder bridge with brick piers set 200ft apart. He later discovered that the river bed was not, as he had hoped, entirely solid rock, so after using brick piers for part of the way, he changed to cast iron columns and the span was increased to 245 ft. The central section was raised to allow shipping to pass safely underneath, by means of gentle gradients on the rest of the bridge on both sides of the raised section. The structure was tested in 1878 by running six heavy locomotives over it. The inspector approved, but suggested not running trains at more than 25mph and added a note that he would have liked to have had an opportunity to see what effect high winds might have on a train crossing the bridge. If that had been possible, the accident might never have happened.

On December 28 !879 those were the weather conditions that the inspector was worried about, with a severe gale blowing down the river. The train set off from St. Fort station on the south side of the river. It never reached Dundee. The whole of the high-level section between piers 28 and 41 had collapsed and the entire train had been lost. It was never exactly determined just how many passengers had been on board, but it was thought to be 75 – they and the train crew all died. There was never any doubt what the official verdict would be. The bridge was described as 'badly designed, badly constructed and badly maintained' and the blame was firmly placed on Bouch. His career was over. Today, many people know only of this tragedy from the excruciatingly bad verses written after the event by William McGonagall. They will not be quoted here as they tend to be regarded as a joke – and there was nothing amusing about the events of that night.

A disaster comparable to that of the Tay Bridge occurred on 29 December in America. The Pacific express, a train consisting of two locomotives and eleven cars had left Erie in the early evening heading towards Cleveland. By the time it had reached Ashtabula the driver was faced with driving snow that, in the darkness, reduced visibility to a just a few yards. Just outside the station it had to cross a 150ft iron truss bridge over a ravine. In an echo of the Dee

The Tay railway bridge as seen from the north bank. The raised section seen in the distance collapsed during a storm in 1879 while a train was crossing.

bridge accident, the driver of the first locomotive heard a cracking noise and opened the regulator to clear the bridge. But again, the connection to the tender broke, and the second engine turned and fell with the collapsing bridge, carrying the entire train with it. To make matters worse, the passenger carriages were all heated by stoves, and within minutes the coaches were ablaze. Amazingly there were survivors and the passengers in the last carriage were especially fortunate: the African-American porter called Steward, finding the carriage on its side, smashed a window and crawled out and then made his way down the rest of the carriage, breaking more windows and pulling out the passengers. Others were less fortunate. Because of the fire it was difficult to work out how many had died, but it was estimated 92 died and many more were injured.

It is rare to have accounts of accidents from those involved, but we do have one describing what happened when a train derailed near Staplehurst on the South Eastern Railway. Repairs were being carried out on a modest viaduct and the men responsible were expecting to complete the work in the gap between two trains, one at 2.51 in the afternoon, the other

The aftermath of the Pacific express disaster.

at 4.14. As a safety precaution, one workman was supposed to be situated 1,000 yards away from the bridge and to lay fog detonators at 250 yard intervals in case the driver failed to see his red flag. But he was only half that distance from the viaduct and was only given two detonators and told not to bother to use them unless it became foggy. Tragically, the maintenance crew had got their timings wrong and when the Folkestone express arrived, one section of rail was still missing. The result was inevitable: the train was derailed and most of it finished in the ditch below the viaduct. One coach, however, remained upright and among its passengers was Charles Dickens. He described what happened in the compartment he was sharing with his young female companion and an older lady. As a novelist the account is, of course, given its full dramatic colour.

> Soddenly we were off the rail, and beating the ground as the car of a half-emptied balloon might. The old lady cried out 'My God!' and the young one screamed. I caught hold of them

The accident at Stapleton in which Charles Dickens was involved as a passenger.

> both (the old lady sat opposite and the young one on my left) and said: 'We can't help ourselves, but we can be quiet and composed. Pray don't cry out.' The old lady immediately answered: 'Thank you. Rely upon me. Upon my soul I will be quiet.' We were then all tilted down together in a corner of the carriage, and stopped. I said to them thereupon, 'You may be sure nothing worse can happen. Our danger *must* be over. Will you remain here without stirring, while I get out of the window?' They both answered quite collectedly 'Yes' and I got out without the least notion what had happened.
>
> Fortunately I got out with great caution and stood upon the step. Looking down I saw the bridge gone, and nothing below but the line of rail. Some people in two other compartments were madly trying to plunge out of the window, and had no idea there was an open swampy field below them and nothing else!

Dickens helped with the rescue effort, but he faced a terrible scene. He fetched his brandy flask from the carriage and took his hat and filled it with water.

> Suddenly I came upon a staggering man covered with blood (I think he must have been flung clean out of his carriage), with such a frightful cut across the skull that I couldn't bear to look at him. I poured some water over his face and gave him some drink, and then gave him some brandy, and laid him down upon the grass, and he said: 'I am gone', and died afterwards. Then I stumbled over a lady lying on her back against a little pollard-tree, with the blood streaming over her face (which was lead colour) in a number of distinct little streams from her head. I asked her if she could swallow a little brandy and she just nodded, and I gave her some and left her for somebody else … No imagination can conceive the ruin of the carriages, or the extraordinary weights under which the people were lying, or the complications into which they were twisted up among iron and wood, and mud and water.

There were many different causes of accidents. In some countries, there was a very real danger of running into large,

In January 1901, the Orient Express jumped the rails at Frankfurt's Central Station and ended up in the restaurant hall; amazingly no one was seriously injured.

wild animals. The first trains to cross the American prairies, for example, had to contend with huge herds of buffalo – hence the 'cow catchers' that were such a feature of the front of American locomotives. That problem almost totally vanished thanks to the buffalo hunters who arrived in the area by train and slaughtered the herds almost to the point of total extinction.

Some accidents were definitely due to driver error, passing signals at stop – or simply failing to stop in time. There is, however, as far as I can see, only one accident that was caused by driver error that involved a member of a royal family on the footplate. The London *Times* of 31 October 1934 had a heroic story of how King Ferdinand of Bulgaria had rushed to help save the life of a driver on the Orient Express. It does not, however, say anything about how he came to need rescuing in the first place. The king was a true railway enthusiast who preferred travelling on the footplate to sitting in a luxury coach and frequently took over from the driver. On this occasion the train was behind schedule and the king was determined to make up time. He kept urging the fireman to heap ever more coal into the firebox until the pressure gauge showed there was a real danger of explosion. The professional driver let off some steam and the pressure dropped back down, but still the king urged the fireman on. He had no choice but to obey the royal command, opened the firebox door and flames burst out, engulfing him – he fell, his clothes ablaze. The king certainly helped put out the flames, but that done, he simply went back to the controls and the train carried on its way, with few if any passengers aware of exactly what had happened.

Some of the worst accidents in railway history were not due to any fault of the railway system or its employees. In June 1989 two Russian trains were approaching each other in the Ural Mountains. They were going to and coming from a holiday resort on the Black Sea and both trains had many children on board who had been camping. What no one knew was that there was a leak from a nearby liquid gas pipe, and it had formed a mist in the gulley where the trains were passing. It is presumed that it was a spark from a wheel, but whatever caused it there was an immense explosion with a huge fireball that was visible for miles. The official figures gave the death toll as 575 of whom 181 were children, but many believe there were even more killed. A doctor who attended the scene reported that it was so horrendous that his normally dark hair had turned grey by the next day.

The worst recorded catastrophe of all happened in Sri Lanka in December 2004. An earthquake out at sea caused a tsunami that swept across the south west coast of the island. The Queen of the Sea train with an estimated 1,700 passengers was simply swept away to disappear under the waves.

The accidents listed here are only a small proportion of the railway accidents that have happened around the world in the last 200 years. It might seem that travelling by train is a hazardous affair to be avoided, but as mentioned at the beginning of the chapter, rail travel is actually one of the safest ways of getting from place to place. In the next chapter we shall be turning away from these scenes of catastrophes to a world were mayhem and skulduggery may be rife but where no one actually gets hurt – the world of fiction.

Chapter 11

RAIL JOURNEYS IN FICTION

It seems that rail journeys have a particular fascination for writers of crime novels. Even in some of the earliest crime stories, notably those featuring Conan Doyle's detective Sherlock Holmes and his friend Dr Watson, many times involve taking trains, the most famous of which is *The Hound of the Baskervilles.* Probably the best-known detective novel set on board a train, however, has to be Agatha Christie's *Murder on the Orient Express,* published in 1934. It has been filmed more than once, though most would agree that the best version is the one featuring Albert Finney as the detective Hercule Poirot and an impressive list of star actors as the various suspects. The train becomes trapped in the snow, so that it becomes the equivalent of the classic country house murder, where the suspects are limited by being the only ones present. The victim, a particularly unpleasant American, is found stabbed twelve times and there are appear to be twelve people on board who all have a motive for hating the man. It is then up to Poirot to sort out which, if any, is the guilty party – a task, needless to say which he manages in his own inimitable way.

This was not Christie's first novel set on board a European train. *The Mystery of the Blue Train* (1928) again features Poirot, this time heading for the French Riviera on Le Train Bleu. The victim in this story is an American heiress, Ruth Kettering, who is found strangled in her compartment and her famous and valuable ruby 'Heart of Fire' is missing. The police suspect Ruth's lover, the Comte de la Roche, but as all readers will expect, Poirot disagrees and will inevitably unmask the real villain. The plot has similarities to an earlier short story by Christie, *The Plymouth Express.* Possibly coincidentally, shortly after the Christie book appeared, another novel *Le Mystère du Train Bleu* by Arthur Bermère was published. It features the popular French detective Chantecoq who, rather like Holmes, is a 'master of disguise'. Unlike the Christie book, the action does not actually take place on the train. Instead, the body of the victim is found on the tracks – he had been shot and then hit by Le Train Bleu. So, the title is a little misleading.

Even before Christie's famous novel appeared, the Orient Express had featured in another novel with both murder and espionage in the lurid mix. Graham Greene's *Stamboul Train* was published in 1931, one of his books to which he gave the name 'entertainment' rather than dignifying them as serious novels. It was Greene's first successful novel and deals with a disparate group of characters on a three day journey on the famous train from Ostend to Istanbul. These include a young female dancer on her way to work in Istanbul and a calculating businessman who seduces her. There is a communist leader travelling on a forged passport hoping to lead a revolution in Serbia and a lesbian journalist who is later robbed by a man who has just committed a murder. As one can imagine with such a cast there are endless possibilities for the mayhem and skulduggery that duly ensue.

One of the mystery stories that would have particular appeal to railway enthusiasts is *The Necropolis Railway* (2005) by Andrew Martin. The railway of the title is an actual line that ran from Waterloo Station, London to a new cemetery that had been built at Brookwood in Surrey. This strange line had trains consisting of both conventional carriages for mourners and other visitors and special hearse carriages for coffins. The story is set in 1903 and the protagonist is a young enthusiastic railwaymen, Jim Stringer who has been recruited from a job at the Robin Hood's Bay station in Yorkshire to work as an engine cleaner at Waterloo. He soon discovers that he is replacing a cleaner who has mysteriously disappeared and more murders occur – all seemingly connected to the railway of the title. The author has been meticulous in his research and presents an accurate picture of the working life of the railways in the Edwardian era. The book was a success and in later volumes, Stringer has left his old job and been seconded to the railway police, where more mysteries are found for him to solve.

Among the many detectives, amateur and professional, who appear in several novels, one of the more popular has always been Dorothy L. Sayers' Lord Peter Whimsey. He does not generally have a great deal to do with trains – normally travelling in his own suitably luxurious motor accompanied by his valet. However, the plot of one of the murder mysteries, *The Five Red Herrings* of 1931, set in an artistic community in Scotland, hinges on railways and railway timetables. A colleague told me that his father, who enjoyed the book, took the trouble to do some research and checked all the timings in the book with genuine timetables of the period – and all were a perfect match. Miss Sayers had done her homework.

Most of the train mystery stories concern events on trains, but Paula Hawkins' best seller of 2015 *The Girl on the Train* is centred on events seen from the train by a depressed, alcoholic young woman when passing the house where she once lived. There is murder, but it is also about complex webs of lies and deceits as told by three different women.

After so much bloodshed, perhaps it is time to turn to something altogether more gentle and one of the best-loved of all railway inspired novels, *The Railway Children* (1906) by E. Nesbit. The story begins when the father of the three children, who works for the Foreign Office, is falsely accused of spying and imprisoned. The family have to move out to a house in the country near a railway, where the children regularly gather to wave to the passing trains and where they make friends with the railwayman Albert Perks at the local station. Events include the arrival of a Russian émigré escaping persecution from the Czarist forces who is taken in by the family and the saving of a catastrophe by stopping the train before it hits a landslip on the line. When they rescue a boy with an injured leg, who was at risk of being run over by a train, the boy's grandfather takes an interest in their father's case and all ends happily. The book was made into a TV series and later into a film, both of which were shot on the preserved Keighley and Worth Valley Railway. Passengers on the line can see the house from which the children ran to see the train in the film and Oakworth station where they befriended Perks. There is another literary connection with

Oakworth station on the Keighley & Worth Valley Railway became the station where the railway children met Albert Perks.

this line, for one of the stations is at Haworth, home to the Bronte sisters and their brother Branwell, who for a time had a job as a railway clerk.

Of all the books written featuring railway travel, few have been more successful than a set that began as bedtime stories for a young boy. The Rev. W. Awdry's son Christopher had a wooden model locomotive that was to become Thomas the Tank Engine. Awdry's wife persuaded him to publish the stories, and for the second book of the series, the illustrator Reginald Payne was called in and the model chosen for Thomas was an 0-6-0 Class E2 tank of the London, Brighton & South Coast Railway. As well as delighting children with the books, Thomas and his friends have also appeared in a TV series. Several preserved railways have benefitted over the years by having Thomas Days, when a tank engine with Thomas's face has been a huge attraction.

One of the first films to tell a story was the Edison movie *The Great Train Robbery* of 1903. It has a simple tale to tell and takes just about a quarter of an hour to tell it. Two bandits come into the railroad office, tie up the telegraph operator and when the train stops to take on water, get on board. There they shoot the guard and blow open a box of valuables. There is a fight on the train tender with the fireman, and then the driver stops the train – the passengers are robbed and the thieves leave on the engine and further down the line they leave to rejoin their horses. The telegraph operator is found and there is a curious interlude of a square dance before the operator bursts in and organises a posse. The bandits are found and killed in a gunfight. The actual filming is primitive, but it is of some interest to railway enthusiasts as it provides a rare chance to see film of a locomotive of the time at work. Anyone interested can find the entire film on line on YouTube. It was the first of many Westerns featuring train robberies, such as *Butch Cassidy and the Sundance Kid* and *Cat Ballou.* The oddest must surely be *Red Sun* of 1971 that manages to combine the traditional Western with a samurai movie. The Japanese ambassador is robbed of a valuable samurai sword while travelling by train through Arizona. His Japanese bodyguard, played by Toshiro Mifune, famous as the star of the great Kurosawa move *Seven Samurai,* sets off in pursuit of the thieves.

As with the books, so thrillers became a popular form of cinema, and no one exploited the genre to better effect than Alfred Hitchcock. Trains played a central role in many of his movies. In 1936, he directed a loose adaptation of John Buchan's novel *The Thirty Nine Steps.* At the start of the film, the hero Richard Hannay helps a young woman, who turns out to be a spy with knowledge of a criminal organisation who plan to steal military secrets. She is murdered in his flat and he is the obvious suspect but is determined to follow up her lead and takes the train to Scotland. In a typical Hitchcock manner, the viewer could simply be given a sight of him boarding the train and then the story would move on to the next bit of action. Instead, we have a comic scene where Hannay shares a compartment with two salesmen discussing their lines in women's corsets. When the police board the train, Hannay escapes and hides among the girders of the Famous Forth bridge. In a later film version, Hannay hides under the less spectacular bridge that carries the Severn Valley Railway over the river.

Two years later he directed *The Lady Vanishes* in which almost all the action takes place on a train heading from a ski resort to connect with the ferry to England. A young woman, played by Margaret Lockwood, has a friendly chat with an elderly lady, Miss Froy, but when she returns to the carriage, the lady has vanished and others in the compartment deny she ever existed. A young musicologist, played by Michael Redgrave, joins the hunt for the missing person. Other passengers fail to help, including two very English gentlemen who are worried that if anything has gone wrong the train might be held up and they will miss a test match. Eventually

A scene aboard the train from *The Lady Vanishes* with Michael Redgrave and Margaret Lockwood, reproduced in the *National Board of Film Reviewers Magazine of 1938*.

we discover that the elderly lady is a British spy and that she is being held by agents from an enemy power. There follows a struggle to find Miss Froy but eventually after a gun fight she makes her escape.

Hitchcock left the British film industry and settled in Hollywood, where trains again featured in his movies. *Strangers on a Train* (1951) is based on a novel by Patricia Highsmith. The two strangers are a wealthy psychotic, Bruno Antony and tennis player Guy Haines. Bruno wants to see his father dead so that he can inherit and discovers that Guy is unhappily married. He suggests swapping murders – he will kill the wife at a time when Guy has a perfect alibi and in return Guy will murder the father. Guy does not take the idea seriously – until his wife is murdered and Bruno demands the reciprocal murder. The rest of the movie is concerned with Guy's attempts to clear his own name and bring Bruno to justice. One other Hitchcock film features a memorable train journey. In *North by North West* (1959) Cary Grant plays a businessman who gets mistaken for a spy, and is soon embroiled with foreign agents and mistakenly accused of murder. He has to disguise himself as a railway porter in order to get away on a train with Eve Marie Saint's character, who is acting as a double agent. The two are united at the end and the last scene has them in a sleeping car on another train – and the finale is an outrageously cheeky visual metaphor.

Perhaps the most unusual thriller featuring a passenger train was set not on the normal railway but on the New York Subway. *The Taking of Pelham 123* was a successful book and made into a movie in 1974 and then remade again in 2009. Four men in identical disguises join the train and then produce weapons and take the passengers hostage. They demand $1 million from the city – money to be paid within an hour or they start shooting hostages. The *New Yorker* reviewer was upset by the 'dirty words used for giggly shock effect' – words that have, for better or worse, become commonplace on screens today.

These are just a sample of the thrillers set on trains and trains also turn up in some memorable comedies. One of the earliest and certainly one of the best of silent comedies featuring trains is *The General* (1926) starring the great Buster Keaton. It is based on an actual event in the American Civil War, described in more detail on p.160. Keaton plays an engine driver in love with Annabelle, who rejects him because she thinks he has refused to join the army – when he had actually been turned down as he was needed more as an engine driver. Union soldiers steal his Confederate locomotive, *The General,* and intend to use it to damage the Confederate rail system. In the process, they also unwittingly take Annabelle with them. Keaston sets off in pursuit to reclaim the engine and Annabelle. The scenes include a splendid train chase. The actual locomotive stolen by the Unionists is preserved and currently on display at the railway and civil war museum in Keneshaw, Georgia.

In the 1930s, a new type of comic film appeared, known as 'screwball comedies'. They featured fast, witty dialogue

The General, the actual locomotive that was captured by Union troops in the American Civil War and was the basis for the movie of the same name. It is now in the railway museum at Kenesaw, Georgia.

and often bizarre plots. Some of the finest were directed by Howard Hawks, among which was *Twentieth Century* starring John Barrymore and Carole Lombard. The plot has Barrymore as a theatre director who takes a dizzy blonde model with no experience and transforms her into the star of his new play. The plot then moves on three years to the point when she decides to leave him for Hollywood. She departs on *The Twentieth Century*, where most of the remaining action takes place. Barrymore, now all but bankrupt, disguises himself to join the train and the rest of the film concerns his frantic efforts to get her to sign a new contract. Another great comedy by a master director, in this case Billy Wilder, is also partly set on a train in the thirties, but *Some Like it Hot* was made in 1959. Two musicians have the misfortune to witness a gangland murder and need to escape town as fast as they can. The only job available is in an all-girl band, so they have to transform themselves into Daphne and Josephine. There is a lengthy sequence on board the train heading to Florida which includes Sugar (Marilyn Monroe) singing *Running Wild* and a party in the sleeping car – an all-time classic comedy.

Leaving America for Britain and going back to the Thirties is the comedy *Oh Mr. Porter* (1937). Will Hay plays an incompetent stationmaster who is posted off to Northern Ireland and the fictional, chaotic station of Buggleskelly. He and the equally incompetent station staff become embroiled with gun runners. Although set in Ireland, the station where much of the film was shot was actually Cliddesdon station on the Basingstoke and Alton Light Railway and the main locomotive featured was No. 2 *Northiam*, a 2-4-0 tank on loan from the Kent & East Sussex Railway.

The Titfield Thunderbolt was a film of 1953 that was directly inspired by the railway preservation movement, in particular the work of volunteers on the Talyllyn Railway. The villagers of Titfield are horrified to hear that their local branch line is to be closed and decide to run it themselves. They are given a month in which to prove to the inspectorate that they can do the job efficiently. Opposing them is the owner of the local bus company. The comedy revolves round their efforts to beat the deadline, which involves acquiring a veteran locomotive

The spectacular accident at the Gare Montmartre in 1897 that was recreated in the movie *Hugo*.

from the local museum. The engine used in the film was, indeed, a genuine veteran. *Lion* was bult for the Liverpool & Manchester Railway in 1837. The Titfield station was actually Monkton Combe on a recently closed branch of the Bristol & North Somerset Railway, which was specially opened for a short time for the filming.

Hugo (2011) is a film directed by Martin Scorsese with most of the action taking place in the Gare Montparnasse in Paris. Hugo is a young boy, whose father, who had been making an automaton, dies. He goes to live with his uncle who maintains the station clock. When the uncle disappears, the boy continues the maintenance work and hides out in the clock tower, while trying to avoid the station inspector.

The refreshment waiting room at Carnforth. It has been restored to look as it did in the film *Brief Encounter*.

In trying to complete the work on the automaton he comes into contact with the great innovator of the silent era, Georges Méliès and eventually helps to organise a showing of the old films. The locomotive featured in the movie was on loan from the Nene Valley Railway as were the wagons-lits. In the film there is a recreation of a famous accident, in which a train crashed through the station wall and ended up, nose down on the pavement. The real accident, however happened in 1897.

The prize for the best romantic film with a railway setting must surely go to *Brief Encounter*, 1945. Based on a play by Noel Coward it tells of the affair between a respectable but bored middle class married Englishwoman, Celia Johnson and an equally unhappily married doctor, Trevor Howard, who meet in a railway station refreshment room. Although known as Milford Junction in the film, it was actually shot at Carnforth, and thanks to the continuing popularity of the film, the Carnforth refreshment room – now the Brief Encounter Bistro - has been restored to look as it did in the 1940s. The film was shot just as Britain was about to go to war – and war will be the themes of the next chapter.

Chapter 12

THE RAILWAYS AT WAR

It must have been obvious, once the railway systems had developed, that trains would be extremely useful in troop and armament movement, being far and away the fastest form of transport available. The reverse of that was that an enemy would regard railways as legitimate targets. Both elements were to appear in wartime. This chapter will not contain accounts of every war in which railways played a significant role – that would require a whole book – but will look at selected conflicts to give an overall impression of how the role of railways in warfare changed over the years.

The first European war in which railways made an effective appearance was during the British siege of Sevastopol in the Crimean War in 1855. The troops were camped on a ridge above the town, but there were enormous difficulties in getting essential supplies to them from the nearest port, nearly five miles away. The only access was via a dirt road which was often so deep in mud that the pack animals died under the strain and the cavalry were actually using their own chargers to help get the essentials to the troops. Even then, as Henry Clifford, one of the officers at the siege reported, men were only getting half or even quarter rations. Morton Peto, the highly successful railway contractor, was also a Member of Parliament and he suggested to the prime minister, Lord Palmerston, that the answer was a railway, which he offered to build with his partner Edward Betts without any payment for themselves. They put out a call for navvies to join the expedition to the Crimea and soon the first detachment was ready to leave from Liverpool with 300 navvies, 100 carpenters, 30 masons, 30 blacksmiths and 12 engine drivers. Along with them went three doctors and two scripture readers. The ship was laden with sleepers and rails and tarpaulins for the men to sleep on until wooden huts were erected. Locomotives followed later.

A print from the *Illustrated London News* showing navvies at work constructing the railway for the British army at Balaclava in the Crimean War.

Many of the army officers were at first unimpressed by the whole enterprise and looked down on the navvies. Captain Henry Clifford described them as 'unutterable things' and added: 'I wish they would make us a good road, for I have little faith in the proposed Railway'. A week later he had completely changed his view, when he was astonished by the progress. The navvies, he wrote 'do more work in a day than a Regiment of English Soldiers do in a week'. An example of just what could be achieved was the construction of a bridge over a stream. A pile driver had been landed off a supply ship in the afternoon and taken in pieces to the site. Within 24 hours, the piles had been driven, the bridge completed and the rails moved on another 100 yards. Everything was completed well ahead of time, and supplies moved freely, but perhaps not as freely as they might have done. The Commissariat introduced regulations that no supplies could be sent before 8am or after 5.30 in the evening. The Army, who had scoffed at the navvies when they first arrived, now wanted them to stay on to build fortifications, but the contractors insisted that they had done their job and were not there simply to serve the military. The railway transformed the situation and in September 1855, the fortress fell to the British.

Although the Crimean railway was important, it played only a small part in the overall campaign. The first war in which rail transport played a key role was the American Civil War. In previous wars, battles tended to be fought near heavily populated areas which could supply the armies' needs. With the widespread rail network this was no longer a problem – supplies could come by train. The war was being fought mainly in the South, and the Unionists recognised the importance of the railways and specifically targeted important rail junctions. When General Sherman led his forces against Atlanta, Georgia, he was entirely reliant on the railways for supply. He later recorded that over a period from 1 May to 12 November 1864, it provided the army with material that he reckoned would have taken 36,800 wagons, each hauled by six mules to bring by road every day. Once they arrived at Atlanta, the Union army began systematically destroying the rail network that led back to Chattanooga, Tennessee, to deny the Confederate army an essential supply line. The destruction was thorough. Rails were heated, then bent round trees into a loop to make them unusable – they became known as 'Sherman's neckties'. It was not only rails that were destroyed, the whole of the Atlanta railroad station was left in ruins. Meanwhile the Union forces were able to defend their own supply lines, bringing men and material to the battlefields and taking the wounded away for treatment. The Confederacy had a more complex system than the North as not every state had the same gauge, some having the standard 4ft 8½in gauge while others were 5ft, making long range movements slower where everything had to be changed from one section to the next.

One of the more famous escapades was mentioned in the previous chapter, known variously as Andrews' Raid or the great locomotive chase. In northern Georgia in April !862, a group of volunteer Union soldiers led by a civilian scout, James Andrews, grabbed the locomotive *The General* and set off towards Chattanooga destroying track and infrastructure as they went and cutting the telegraph wires, which meant that the Confederate troops along the way could not be told what was happening, and simply assumed it was one of their own trains as it passed them by. Forces set off in pursuit at first on foot and horseback, but later with locomotives. The Confederates eventually caught up with the train and, because the men were in Confederate uniforms, they were treated as spies and executed, including the civilian Andrews. What is not so well known is that this was not the first such attempt. Andrews had led an earlier expedition. It had been reported that a train driver in Georgia was prepared to defect and would drive his train north if he could have a crew of Unionists to assist him. The expedition set off on foot to Tullahoma, where they were able to travel on by train. However, when they reached Marietta, where they were to meet the driver, they discovered he had been posted away to another depot. No one in the party knew how to drive an engine, so there was nothing to be done but to return to the

The locomotive *The General* that had been hijacked by Union soldiers who drove it south towards Chattanooga destroying bridges as they went.

Union lines. It was an extraordinarily dangerous affair, and they were nearly captured when cutting telegraph wires, but managed to persuade the troops they were carrying out essential repairs. None of those who took part on this attempted train capture volunteered for the second raid – it was, they felt, pushing their luck a bit too far.

Shortly after the end of the American Civil War, Europe was also to see a major conflict. In 1870, France went to war with Prussia and again the railways had a vital role to play. Both sides began to mobilise their troops. The French relied on just one railway company to carry men to the front line, the Compagnie de l'Est. They managed to move 186,000 men, 32,000 horses and 4,000 artillery pieces. The Prussians had a far more complex system to negotiate, involving several different rail companies and many lengths of single track. Their planning, however, was immaculate and in the same time as the French were moving their troops, they were able to bring more than twice as many, roughly 400,000 men, to the front. The French suffered an early, major defeat at the Battle of Sedan, during which the Emperor Napoleon III was captured, but two fortresses held out at Reims and Metz. They controlled essential sections of track that prevented the Prussians advancing on Paris. The Prussians now had long lines of communication, and the French did what they could to harass them, damaging the track and on one occasion managing to blow up a troop train. The end, however, came soon and an armistice was agreed just six months from the start in Paris in January 1871. One novel feature of the war was the use of carriages and wagons as field hospitals for the wounded.

The First World War was largely fought in continental Europe. The Schlieffen Plan depended on a rapid movement of troops by rail on two fronts. They would move rapidly through Belgium and Luxembourg and then enter northern France and head for Paris. At this point it was expected that the French would surrender, and the German forces could move onto their next major objective – the invasion of Russia. It looked good on paper, but the resistance in Belgium was not instantly overcome. Much of the essential railway network on which the Germans relied for support

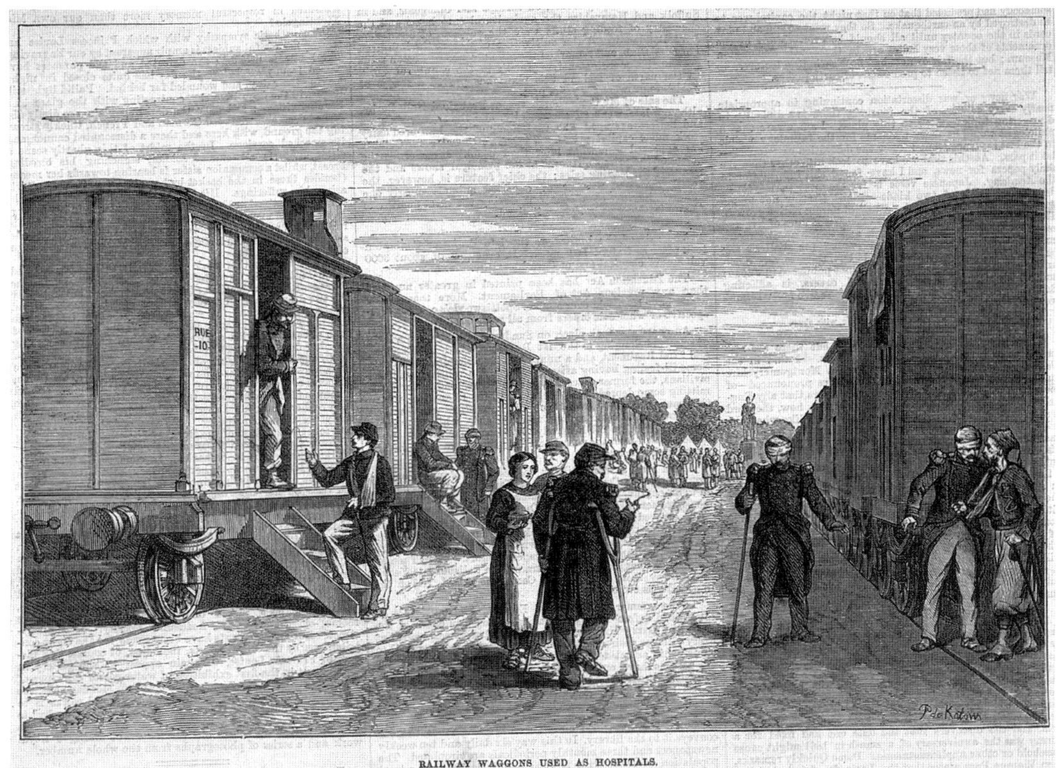

Railway wagons being used as field hospitals during the Franco-Prussian War.

was destroyed. The German troops found themselves around 80 miles from the nearest railhead and had to rely on horses to bridge the gap. The French, with their rail system intact, were able to bring up more forces, and the British began pouring troops across the Channel. Everything ground to a halt at the Western Front, a system of trenches that extended from the Channel to the Swiss border. The war was now characterised by a series of attempts to break the deadlock, usually with huge loss of life and very little change to the positions of the two sides. Communication became the key to bringing up supplies, particularly for the huge artillery offensives that marked both sides on the battlefield.

In mainland Britain, all railways were immediately put under government control through the Regulation of the Forces Act – Irish railways remained independent until 1917. The first essential was to mobilise the British troops of the expeditionary force that would head across the Channel. The railway unions agreed to fully co-operate and in the first month of the war, 760 special troop trains were run. The huge increase in work load produced staff shortages, a problem exacerbated by the number of young men signing up for the army. The answer was to start employing women in jobs that had previously been exclusively male, such as acting as porters, ticket inspectors and later on as railway police. Over 50,000 women were employed altogether, though it was made clear that once the war was over, they would have to give

During the First World War, women took on many jobs that had previously been done by men. Here she is cleaning a Great Central Railway third class carriage.

their jobs up to the returning men. But without their efforts, the railway could simply not have been run.

As the war progressed, or rather failed to progress, as well as the traffic in men and supplies heading for the battlefield, there was a steady increase of traffic in the opposite direction, bringing home the wounded. Special ambulance carriages were designed in the first month of the war, one of which was ordered for the navy from the London & North Western Railway works at Wolverton. Adapted from existing carriages, it was delivered to Chatham within thirty hours of the order being placed, to the delight of the Surgeon General, Sir James Porter, who wrote a letter of thanks:

> Royal Naval Corridor Ambulance Train from Wolverton has arrived to-day and has gladdened me very much. It is so satisfactory that I am asking the Admiralty for a second of similar construction. I consider great praise is due for the manner the department under your care has carried out this work.

The railways had to cope with unprecedented traffic. The Highland line that served the north of Scotland, from Perth to Thurso in the far north was originally carrying as many sheep as passengers, but suddenly the difficult 272 mile route, 230 miles of which were single track, became a major link to the fleet at Scapa Flow. They also served the naval refuelling and repair base at Invergordon, north of Inverness. The local station there was almost overwhelmed with the staff putting in immensely long hours, often starting work at 6am and not finishing until after midnight. The engines were worked almost to destruction with the unexpected heavy loads. By August 1915 the company that had started with 152 engines had to scrap 50, while another 50 were in urgent need of repair. At the end of the war, Sir Herbert A. Walker chairman of the Railway Executive, wrote: 'I think the Highland has been hit harder than any other company.'

All stations were stretched to provide services for the vast numbers of troops being moved. At Perth at the start of the war, women started arriving with baskets of fruit and provided cups of tea for the troops. It was soon decided that

Volunteer women feeding the troops at Victoria Station, London in the First World War.

they needed to organise, and the Perthshire Women's Patriotic Committee was formed, after which they were able to provide a 24-hour service, and a special rest room was made available from 8pm to 1am for men waiting for a connection. Similar groups were formed around the country. When a buffet was opened at Euston run by volunteer women, they were serving as many as 4,000 men in a 24-hour period. Their activity was given a royal seal of approval, when the queen visited shortly after the opening.

The war in Europe was not the only area of conflict. The Ottoman Empire joined in on the German side of the conflict. This was also, however, a period of Arab revolt against the Empire, which received British support. Among the British officers who went to the Middle East, the most famous was T.E. Lawrence – 'Lawrence of Arabia'. He led an Arab group, who undertook several attacks on railways in 1917. In his book *Seven Pillars of Wisdom* (1926) he described one of these attacks. One train had appeared, but for some reason the previously set explosives failed to go off. The explosives were reset and a second train appeared.

> Round the bend, whistling its loudest, came the train, a splendid two-engined thing of twelve passenger coaches, travelling at top speed on the favourable grade. I touched off under the first driving wheel of the first locomotive, and the explosion was terrific. The ground spouted blackly into my face, and I was sent spinning, to sit up with the shirt torn to my shoulder and the blood dripping from long, ragged scratches on my left arm. Between my knees lay the exploder, crushed under a twisted sheet of sooty iron. In front of me was the scalded and smoking upper half of a man. When I peered through the dust and steam of the explosion the whole boiler of the first engine seemed to be missing.

Among the casualties of that attack was the commander of the Eighth Army Corps, who, with the troops on the train, had been on is way to help in the defence of Jerusalem from a British attack.

The Second World War was fought around the globe and again railway communications were vital for the movement of troops and supplies. In Europe, the German offensive swept through France at speed and by May 1940 the British had retreated to the Channel coast and on 27 May the famous evacuation from Dunkirk was begun and completed by 4 June. In that time,338,226 soldiers had arrived in Britain and needed to be taken away to different parts of the country as rapidly as possible. Most of the work of moving them fell to the Southern Railway, with extra coaches being requisitioned from the GWR, LMS and LNER. The great majority were taken from Dover and Folkestone and in just a few days 319,116 troops had been carried in 620 trains It was an extraordinary feat of organisation. It was not the only evacuation programme involving the railways. In the First World War, there had been raids by Zeppelins that caused comparatively little damage, but things in the 1940s were very different. Now German bomber raids created immense damage and thousands of children were evacuated by rail from the main target areas to the comparative safety of rural areas, where they would be

Troops who had just been evacuated from Dunkirk at Dover station.

housed with families who had agreed to take them in. London was a major target, and the London Underground stations became air raid shelters at night during the Blitz. Elsewhere many stations were severely damaged, not just the main line London stations, but others around the country, including Norwich, York and Manchester. Victoria, London, suffered an unexpected damage when a German Dormer bomber brought down by a Hurricane fighter crashed into the forecourt.

In occupied Europe, resistance fighters did their best to sabotage the German war effort by attacking railways. The German attack on Russia depended on a line of communication through Poland and huge disruption was created by the Polish resistance. Over the years they damaged nearly 7,000 locomotives and almost 20,000 trucks. In France, following the D-day landings by allied troops at Normandy, the resistance harassed troop trains bringing up reinforcements to northern France.

The London Underground provided shelter from the bombing during the Second World War.

There are many other stories connected with the railways at this period, some of which are more infamous than famous. The Japanese built the Burmese Railway for their troops using forced labour and prisoners of war, a story that formed the background to the popular film *Bridge on the River Kwai*. But nothing is more horrific than the movement by train of the victims of the holocaust, carried in cattle trucks to the death camps. One of these trucks is now preserved at the Technikmuseum, Berlin. Visitors are allowed to step inside; many, like myself, preferred not to. It would be good to end this chapter by reporting that railways are no longer being attacked in wars, but alas that is not possible. In April 2022, Russian missiles were aimed at the Ukrainian Kramatorsk station, at which thousands of women and children were waiting for trains to take them away from the danger zones. Wars inevitably present contrasts between evil and heroism – the railways were never an exception.

Chapter 13

NOSTALGIA

British Railways' last steam engine was built at the Swindon works in 1960 and was named, after a public discussion, *Evening Star.* It marked the end of steam traction on almost the whole network. Other countries were slower to change and it was a surprise, visiting India in the 1980s, to find all the trains running in and out of the mainline station at Delhi were still steam hauled, though electrification plans were already in hand. But there were still enthusiasts who were not prepared to see the steam age die.

For many of us, the steam engine has a very special, elemental quality – many tons of iron are moved by nothing more than the power of fire and water. In action, a locomotive has its own very special sounds. Knowledgeable enthusiasts can envisage from the noises it makes whether the engine is travelling on the flat or on a gradient and can envisage just what is happening on the footplate. There is the whisper of steam when coasting downhill, the panting up a climb or the regular rhythm of speeding along a level track. On rare occasions, they might hear unwanted, irregular rhythms that suggest all might not be well. That we can still enjoy the delights of the steam railway is mainly down to the work of enthusiasts.

Not every line ended steam running. The Vale of Rheidol Railway is a narrow-gauge line in Wales that from the first was designed both to serve local lead mines and to take visitors to the waterfalls at Devil's Bridge. The lead mines eventually closed but the line was still a popular tourist attraction so there was no need to modernise and the authorities presumably recognised that the steam locomotives were as much a part of the attraction as the scenic falls. The railway was privatised in 1989. A similar story could be told about the Ffestiniog, although it was never in public ownership. Here the slate traffic had steadily diminished as the tourist traffic grew. Both lines are still running and are as popular as ever, combining an irresistible combination of exhilarating scenery and vintage locomotives and rolling stock. But not all the narrow gauge lines seemed likely to survive, especially if their main income had been freight.

The Talyllyn started life in 1863, built to bring slate from the quarries at Bryn Eglwys down to a new port at Tywyn. It was something of an oddity from the start. The first six and three-quarter miles from Tywyn climbed up through the hills to Nant Gwernol and was worked by locomotives, and from there to the quarries there was a mixture of horse-drawn and cable-operated sections. The steam section was also designed for passengers, but when the inspector came to view the line, he decreed that the gap between the carriages and the bridge abutments along the line was too close for safety. The company was disinclined to order new rolling stock, so the company decided to move the rails under the bridges, slightly off centre and permanently close off the carriage doors on the side nearest to the bridge wall. Quite what would happen if the carriages toppled over in a derailment and ended up with the only side with doors at the bottom was not considered an obstacle to a safety certificate being issued. A further speciality of the line was having trucks for hire. A family could be hauled up, wander the hills and perhaps picnic and if they missed the last train back, well, it was all downhill anyway, and the trucks had brakes. Perhaps sadly, for the more adventurous, the trucks for hire business stopped some time ago. So, this was a quirky little line that somehow staggered on into the second half of the twentieth century.

The owner of both mines and quarries, Sir Henry Haydn, maintained a passenger service even after the quarries closed, but when he died his widow understandably was reluctant to take on a rusty track and clapped out locomotives. That would have been that, if the author L.T.C. Rolt had not been walking in the area and fallen in love with the old railway. He called meetings to suggest taking over the line, raised funds and eventually the newly formed Talyllyn Railway Preservation Society was able to acquire the line. There was one major obstacle to overcome; they had to convince the

railway inspectorate that a group of amateurs could run a railway and that the engines were safe to use. They managed to meet both criteria, though it was down to good fortune that when the metalwork of one of the locomotives was tested, the inspector hit one of the few sound pieces on the engine. Today, it is a thriving and delightful line, the first to be taken over and run by a preservation group.

The Talyllyn Railway, the first to be restored and run by volunteers; the train is waiting at the top of the line at Nant Gwernol.

Narrow gauge railways were always at risk, often serving declining industries and running through thinly populated areas. This was just as true in other countries as it was in Britain. In America, the Denver & Rio Grande had a network of these lines in the Rocky Mountains, most of which were abandoned. One line, however, that survived was the Durango and Silverton in Colorado: the clue to why it was built is in the name, Silverton – silver town. It ran three mixed passenger and freight trains a week. The Rio Grande would have liked to close it down, but the Federal Government insisted on it being kept open. Somewhat reluctantly, the company decided to make the best of things and began promoting it as a tourist attraction, beginning by giving their coaching stock an overhaul and providing them with a shiny new bright yellow livery. It must rank among the greatest scenic railways, with a total track length of just over 45 miles and winding its way through the Animas River Canyon, clinging to a narrow ledge on a cliff face and surrounded by mountain peaks. Eventually it was bought out by another company and today carries some 200,000 passengers a year, hauled by coal-fired steam engines.

One other narrow gauge line deserves a special mention. The German Harz Railway in the Harz Mountains is a metre gauge line, that runs for 138km through splendid scenery to eventually reach a summit level at a height of 509m below the 1,142m of the Brocken, the highest peak of the range. It remains almost entirely worked by steam.

The lines we have looked at so far have not only all been narrow gauge, but have all remained more or less in continuous use. Standard gauge lines generally have a rather different history, with one notable exception. The Middleton Colliery Railway has a history that goes right back to the middle of the eighteenth century. In 1758, the colliery owners obtained an Act of Parliament authorising them to build a line from the pit to the Aire & Calder Navigation near Leeds – the first railway ever to receive an enabling Act. For the next half century, the line was worked by horse, but with the price of fodder rocketing thanks to the Napoleonic War, the line's manager John Blenkinsop decided to introduce locomotives. He was aware of the Trevithick pioneering experiments, which had proved that a locomotive could do the job – but he was also aware that the heavy engine had broken the brittle cast iron rails. To get the necessary power with a light engine, he and the local engineer Matthew Murray, came up with the solution – a rack and pinion railway, similar to that now used on mountain railways, except that the rack was outside the running rails not in between them, as horses were still in use and needed a clear way between the rails. Opened in 1812, it was the world's first successful commercial railway. In time, the railway was converted to conventional steam traction and continued in use until 1960, when the pit closed.

The closure of the pit could have been the end of the line as coal had been a major source of revenue. But part of the line was still in use and to keep it open, volunteers from Leeds University offered to run the remaining freight services without payment. As an extra, they also began to run occasional passenger trips. By the 1980s, however, all freight traffic came to an end, but the volunteers were still able to obtain a length of track and offer more regular passenger trips. They now have a visitor centre, where the story of this unique railway is told – nowhere else can chalk up three firsts – first railway Act, first successful commercial steam railway and first preserved standard gauge line. No one would claim it is the most scenic railway, but no other line can boast a continuous history spanning almost three centuries.

Britain today has more preserved steam railways than any other country, largely due to two related factors – the Beeching Reports and Woodhams scrap yard, Barry. In the 1960s, the two reports proposed closing a vast array of unprofitable branch lines and speeding up the change from steam to diesel and electric traction. Thousands of locomotives were sent for scrap, many of them ending up at the Woodhams yard. As a result, a lot of track was redundant but could be made available for volunteers to reuse. At Barry, instead of simply cutting up the engines for reuse by the steel industry, many were saved and were sold for their equivalent scrap value. This was great news for steam enthusiasts and good value for Woodhams, who got their money without having the expense of cutting up the engines. A win-win situation. Today, Britain has more than fifty preserved railways, many of which not only preserve the locomotives and rolling stock, but also maintain stations to look much as they did in the days when steam dominated the railway scene. They also frequently preserve important historical infrastructure such as signal boxes and old-style semaphore signals.

A steam excursion crossing the Ribblehead viaduct on the Settle & Carlisle line.

Today, preserved steam railways are to be found across the world from Europe to Australia, but not all preserved engines run on preserved tracks. Steam excursions have become equally common and very popular. These usually involve special trains made up of vintage carriages headed by one or even two locomotives. Among the most popular are those using particularly well-known engines, such as the recently restored *Flying Scotsman* in Britain. The combination of a spectacular route with a magnificent locomotive can make for an unforgettable experience. One of my earliest excursions was over the famous Settle and Carlisle line behind one of the world's great locomotives, the A4 Pacific *Sir Nigel Gresley* – a member of the same class as the world steam locomotive speed record holder, *Mallard*.

These days, nostalgia has extended beyond the steam age. Many feel equally strongly about preserving older diesel and electric. One of the most exotic, both in its exterior and interior design, is Italy's ETR 252 Arlecchino, an electric train set that made its first appearance in 1960. It is to be hoped that these reminders of the railway past will continue to survive for future generations to enjoy, when no doubt travel will be very different. What, if any, role will the railways play in the next decades?

In the immediate future, railways should be especially valuable in a world threatened by the devastation of global warming, where reducing the use of fossil fuels has to be a priority. Transport systems that move large numbers of people together are far less polluting that moving them in individual vehicles, and this will be true even if we all begin to abandon our petrol and diesel cars in favour of new electric vehicles. With electrification now the norm in many countries, travelling by rail is unquestionably the most environmentally friendly way of getting around a country. That is all very good, but the individual traveller will certainly be looking at other factors, especially price. In Britain today, the train is not the best option. I recently travelled from Bristol to Inverness. If I was to repeat the journey today, I could take a flight for £22.99 single or the train with a cheapest price of £118. Which one are most people going to opt for? In Germany, by contrast, a special summer ticket was issued that allowed rail travel across the entire network for a very modest amount, and in 2023 a new scheme is being rolled out in which for 49 euros you can get unlimited travel on all forms of public transport for a whole month. If a similar system existed in Britain, then my next trip to Inverness would certainly be by train.

Train travel has changed dramatically from the days when the poorer people were squashed into what were little better than open trucks to the high-speed electric trains of today. A railway journey still has its own very special appeal. You do not have to arrive at the station hours before your train is due to leave, unlike passengers travelling by air. Once on board, you can enjoy a degree of comfort for a long journey and can sit back and enjoy the scenery. I have walked

Steam in Australia: the 48-mile long Steam Ranger heritage Railway is a last remanent of the 5ft 3in gauge rail system. The train is headed by Rx Class engine No.224, built in 1915.

from the outskirts of Glasgow to Fort William on the West Highland Way and returned by train. I saw more deer from the train than I did when on foot. Occasionally I have enjoyed wonderful views from the air – a memorable flight over the Alps and another passing quite low, down Manhattan. Most of the time, however, the view has been of the tops of clouds. As for travelling by road – the pleasures of that, in Britain at least, vanished long ago. With luck, the story of travelling by train still has a long way to go.

ACKNOWLEDGEMENTS

The author would like to thank the following for providing illustrations for this book. Others are from out of copyright material or from the author's own collection.

Andy Dingley, p.95; Andrew Bone, p.105; Canadian National Libraries and Archive, p.101; City and County of Swansea, Swansea Museum Collection, p.7; Compagnie Internationals des Wagons-Lits, pp. 75, 76, 77; DB Museum im Verkhersmuseum, Nurnberg' p.30; D. Convertini, p.81; Deben Dave, p.156; Greyghost, p.52; Hassocks, p.96; JEFF BUCK, 173; John Scott Morgan, pp., 93, 94; Louis Figuier, p.71; Patrick Garland, p.104; RAS Marketing, p.96; Royal Commonwealth Institute Library, p.00; Science and Society, p.121; Stephen Richards, p.137; Steve Daniels, p.149; Tennessee State Library and Archive, p.128; Toledo-Lucas County Library, p.39; Tom Page, p.00; Thomas Hemes, p.115; Transport for London, p.118; University of British Columbia Library, p.168; Yair Hekli, p.51; Yagaansh, p.121; Yosemite, p.107

INDEX